# JAMES BUCHANAN

# The Presidents of the United States

George Washington
1789–1797

John Adams
1797–1801

Thomas Jefferson
1801–1809

James Madison
1809–1817

James Monroe
1817–1825

John Quincy Adams
1825–1829

Andrew Jackson
1829–1837

Martin Van Buren
1837–1841

William Henry Harrison
1841

John Tyler
1841–1845

James Polk
1845–1849

Zachary Taylor
1849–1850

Millard Fillmore
1850–1853

Franklin Pierce
1853–1857

James Buchanan
1857–1861

Abraham Lincoln
1861–1865

Andrew Johnson
1865–1869

Ulysses S. Grant
1869–1877

Rutherford B. Hayes
1877–1881

James Garfield
1881

Chester Arthur
1881–1885

Grover Cleveland
1885–1889

Benjamin Harrison
1889–1893

Grover Cleveland
1893–1897

William McKinley
1897–1901

Theodore Roosevelt
1901–1909

William H. Taft
1909–1913

Woodrow Wilson
1913–1921

Warren Harding
1921–1923

Calvin Coolidge
1923–1929

Herbert Hoover
1929–1933

Franklin D. Roosevelt
1933–1945

Harry Truman
1945–1953

Dwight Eisenhower
1953–1961

John F. Kennedy
1961–1963

Lyndon B. Johnson
1963–1969

Richard Nixon
1969–1974

Gerald Ford
1974–1977

Jimmy Carter
1977–1981

Ronald Reagan
1981–1989

George H. W. Bush
1989–1993

William J. Clinton
1993–2001

George W. Bush
2001–2009

Barack Obama
2009–

# James Buchanan

## MICHAEL BURGAN

Other Marshall Cavendish Offices:
Marshall Cavendish International (Asia) Private Limited, 1 New Industrial Road, Singapore 536196 •
Marshall Cavendish International (Thailand) Co Ltd. 253 Asoke, 12th Flr, Sukhumvit 21 Road, Klongtoey
Nua, Wattana, Bangkok 10110, Thailand • Marshall Cavendish (Malaysia) Sdn Bhd, Times Subang, Lot
46, Subang Hi-Tech Industrial Park, Batu Tiga, 40000 Shah Alam, Selangor Darul Ehsan, Malaysia

Marshall Cavendish is a trademark of Times Publishing Limited

All websites were available and accurate when this book was sent to press.

Library of Congress Cataloging-in-Publication Data

Burgan, Michael.
James Buchanan / by Michael Burgan.
p. cm.—(Presidents and their times)
Summary: "Provides comprehensive information on President James Buchanan and places him within
his historical and cultural context. Also explored are the formative events of his times and how he
responded"—Provided by publisher.
Includes bibliographical references and index.
ISBN 978-0-7614-4810-5
1. Buchanan, James, 1791–1868—Juvenile literature.
2. Presidents—United States—Biography—Juvenile literature. I. Title.
E437.B94 2011
973.6'8092—dc22
[B]
2009025933

Editor: Christine Florie
Publisher: Michelle Bisson
Art Director: Anahid Hamparian
Series Designer: Alex Ferrari

Photo research by Thomas Khoo

The photographs in this book are used by permission and through the courtesy of: *Corbis*: 3, 30, 42, 43,
53, 91, 93, 94 (r), 95 (l & r); *Getty Images*: 52, 65; *North Wind Picture Archives*: cover, 6, 68, 80; *Topfoto*:
8, 11, 13, 14, 16, 17, 22, 23, 36, 41, 44, 45, 50, 54, 55, 56, 59, 61, 63, 64, 67, 72, 75, 76, 79, 81, 83, 85,
86, 89, 90, 94 (l).

Printed in Malaysia
1 3 5 6 4 2

# A Troubled President's Early Years

## One

As he became the fifteenth U.S. president on March 4, 1857, James Buchanan knew the country faced difficult times. The issue of slavery had been threatening to divide the North and South for more than two decades. Northern **abolitionists** called for slavery's immediate end across the country. Most Northerners did not seek to abolish slavery where it already existed, but they did want to halt its spread to new territories. Meanwhile, most Southerners, whether they owned slaves or not, defended slavery. They believed it helped the economy of their region. Some Southerners also said slavery provided better conditions for African Americans than freedom could.

At his inauguration, Buchanan said that his election reflected the "love for the Constitution and the Union which still animates the hearts of the American people." Buchanan had spent much of his long career as a public servant defending the Constitution. He believed the country's founding legal document gave the federal government "the specific powers . . . sufficient for almost every possible emergency."

This faith in the Constitution helped explained Buchanan's desire to preserve the **Union**. He knew Southerners had long talked of **secession** because of the increasing attempts to limit slavery. Proslavery forces believed Northerners would not be satisfied with merely halting the spread of slavery. Slaveowners feared that antislavery forces would soon seek to end it everywhere.

Buchanan understood the South's concerns, since the Constitution allowed slavery. But he also believed no state had a constitutional right to secede.

During his inaugural address, Buchanan announced

*Buchanan spent his boyhood in a log cabin, much like this one, one the western frontier of the United States.*

that he would serve only one term. How he handled the slavery issue and the seething anger it stirred across the country would define his presidency.

## A Country Boy

James Buchanan began his long road to the presidency in a log cabin. He was born on April 23, 1791, at Stony Batter, near a pass in the Allegheny Mountains in Cove Gap, Pennsylvania. Buchanan's parents had ten children, all but one of whom survived infancy.

The family's home in a remote backwoods spot might suggest that the Buchanans were poor, but James Buchanan Sr. did well as a merchant. He had come to America from Ireland in 1783, though his family's roots were in Scotland. By the time James Jr. was born, Mr. Buchanan owned a trading post located on a hundred-acre farm with several barns, stables, and an orchard. A few years later he bought Dunwoodie Farm in nearby Mercersburg. This tract of land was three times as big as the Stony Batter farm.

Like her husband, Elizabeth Speer Buchanan, mother of the future president, was Scotch-Irish. Born in Pennsylvania, she was a self-educated woman who could quote famous English writers from memory. She was also a member of the Presbyterian Church. Mrs. Buchanan raised young James and her other children in this faith, and she served as their first teacher. As an adult, James Buchanan wrote that his mother "excited [my] ambition, by presenting . . . in glowing colors men who had been useful to their country." Mrs. Buchanan particularly loved to tell her children about the heroism of George Washington, who became the first U.S. president just two years before James was born.

## THE SCOTCH-IRISH

The Scotch-Irish (also called Scots-Irish) were among the most important immigrant groups to settle in eighteenth-century America. They played a key role in the early political life of the United States. Starting in the late sixteenth century, the English government encouraged the Scotch to settle in Northern Ireland. They took over land that had belonged to the local Irish Catholics. Over time, the Scotch-Irish came to dislike England's restrictions on their own religion, the Protestant Presbyterian denomination. Many also struggled to survive in their new home. During the early 1700s, the Scotch settlers in Ireland began moving to America by the thousands and brought their faith with them. Many settled in Pennsylvania, where colonial law allowed freedom of religion. Buchanan was one of several Scotch-Irish presidents. Others during his lifetime included Andrew Jackson and James K. Polk.

When James was six, the Buchanans moved to a larger stone house in Mercersburg, while also keeping Dunwoodie Farm. The new home included the family store on the first floor, and James Buchanan Sr. continued to thrive in his business. With his profits, he bought land all over town, and by some accounts he was the richest man in Mercersburg.

During his years in Mercersburg, young James worked in his father's store. He learned bookkeeping, as his father watched closely to make sure his son recorded the numbers correctly. The future president never lost the habit of carefully tracking all the money he spent and received.

As the Buchanan family grew, James, who was the only son for most of his childhood, was pressed by his father to prepare for the family business. Mr. Buchanan stressed hard work in the store and on the farm as a way to achieve success. He expected his son to work hard, too. Mr. Buchanan loved his son, but rarely offered praise for James's hard work. Mrs. Buchanan, however, more readily showed her affection, and James also received loving attention from his sisters.

## OFF TO SCHOOL

James began his formal schooling in Mercersburg. The town did not have a public school, so he attended the Old Stone Academy, a private school. Like most boys of the era, James studied Greek and Latin. (At the time, few girls attended school outside the home.) Reading classic books written in these ancient languages was considered the foundation of a good education. James also learned some math and history. James excelled in school, and in 1807 his family decided to send him to college.

At sixteen, he entered the fourteen-student junior class at Dickinson College, in Carlisle, Pennsylvania; the entire school had barely forty-two teens. Mr. Buchanan hoped that James would become a lawyer.

At Dickinson James's courses once again included Latin, Greek, math, and history, along with geography, litera-

*Public elementary schools did not become common across the United States until long after Buchanan finished his schooling.*

ture, and philosophy. James did well with his course work, but the other students thought that anyone who studied too much was a bore. Hoping to avoid such a label, Buchanan later wrote that "to be considered a clever and spirited youth, I engaged in every sort of extravagance and mischief."

The wild adventures caught up with him in September 1808. As James prepared to go back to Dickinson for his second and final year, Mr. Buchanan received a letter from the school. The president was expelling James because of his actions the previous year. The president said the school had considered James a problem for some time but had delayed expelling him because of Mr. Buchanan's fine reputation. An angry James Sr. silently gave his son the letter, to read for himself. The news stunned young James.

The elder Buchanan turned to the family's minister for help. The clergyman knew the leaders of Dickinson and convinced them to let James return. Relieved, James worked hard in school and won an award. But he was not satisfied with the award process itself and tried to change it. To the professors at Dickinson, this was another sign of the arrogance that had dismayed them before. Everyone knew that James was an excellent student, but he seemed to think his abilities put him above others. To show their displeasure, the teachers took away James's award, which angered him. His father, however, saw the loss of the award as a learning experience: James would have to accept the disappointment and get over it.

By graduation day, the flaring tempers on all sides began to cool. The professors would not let James speak first—the honor given to the top student—but he would be able to deliver a speech he had written. Still, as the years went on, James did not have fond memories of his time at Dickinson.

## YOUNG LAWYER

Leaving Dickinson with his degree, young Buchanan headed to Lancaster, the capital of Pennsylvania at the time. He had made arrangements to work for and study with James Hopkins, considered to be one of the best lawyers in the state. At the time, the United States had only one law school. Most young men learned the law from experienced lawyers, studying from their books and helping them prepare their cases.

Buchanan tried to impress Hopkins with his desire to succeed. The young man read law codes and cases that involved the U.S. Constitution, as well as the writings of important legal scholars. The years working with Hopkins shaped Buchanan's beliefs in the importance of obeying the Constitution and following legal precedents—the earlier decisions on a particular point of law. Just as with his detailed bookkeeping, Buchanan paid careful attention to gathering all the facts and using them in a logical way.

In 1812, with his studies over, Buchanan passed an informal interview and was then able to practice law. He opened his own small office in Lancaster and began taking on students. He also received an assignment arguing cases for the county government.

Buchanan worked hard, just as he had in school. He handled legal duties across the area of southern Pennsylvania west of Philadelphia. The work included writing wills and sorting out competing claims over land. Like his father before him, Buchanan also acquired property. He and a partner bought a tavern that also had room for Buchanan's law office.

## AT WAR

When Buchanan started his law practice in Lancaster, the United States was at war. Since the early 1800s, British warships had been engaging in impressment—the forced removal of American

*As a young lawyer, Buchanan sought cases that would bring him public attention.*

sailors from their ships. The British claimed that the sailors were actually deserters from the British navy, and in some cases this was true. Other impressed sailors, however, were U.S. citizens. Presidents Thomas Jefferson and James Madison demanded an end to impressment, as well as free passage of U.S. ships to any port they chose, for Great Britain was restricting American access to certain ports as part of its ongoing war with France.

In June 1812 the conflicts at sea led Congress to declare war on Great Britain. The War of 1812 is sometimes called the second war for independence. The Americans wanted to stand up to the much more powerful British and assert their rights as an independent nation.

President Madison belonged to the **Democratic Republican Party**, as did most members of Congress who supported the war. The other political party of the day, the **Federalists**, opposed the war. The Federalists tended to favor good relations with Great Britain and feared greater disruption of trade. Federalists in New York and New England also knew that Canada would be a target in the war, and they did not want fighting so close to their borders.

*During the 1800s, the British forced American sailors to leave their ships and serve on British vessels.*

# THE FIRST PARTIES

The first U.S. political parties emerged over the fight to ratify, or approve, the Constitution, and then took more solid shape in Congress during the presidency of George Washington. Supporters of the Constitution were called Federalists, and their opponents were the Antifederalists. During the 1790s Alexander Hamilton emerged as the leader of the Federalists. Hamilton was Washington's first secretary of the Treasury. He supported a strong national government and a federal bank that could help industry and trade grow. Opposing Hamilton was Secretary of State Thomas Jefferson. As head of the department that handles foreign relations, the secretary of state is also traditionally considered the most important of the president's advisers. Together, these department heads form a president's **cabinet**.

The group that formed around Jefferson was called either the Democratic Party or the Jeffersonian Republican Party. (This party is distinct from today's Republican Party.) Its members favored a limited federal government and more power for the states. Democratic Republicans also tended to support policies that helped farmers rather than bankers and merchants. By the time Buchanan entered politics, the Federalists had lost much of their power, except in the Northeast. During the War of 1812, some New England Federalists so opposed the war that they threatened to secede.

Buchanan, like his father, was a Federalist. Although most Federalists opposed the war, when the fighting got close to Lancaster, Buchanan was ready to do his part. In August 1814, British troops came ashore in Virginia and marched to Washington, D.C.

*British troops march through Washington, D.C., on the night of August 24, 1814, after setting fire to many public buildings.*

The enemy burned down most of the buildings in the capital including the interior of the presidential mansion at 1600 Pennsylvania Avenue (known officially since 1901 as the White House). Residents in neighboring states feared for their safety, not knowing where the British would strike next. On August 25, Buchanan gave his first public speech: a call for volunteers to join him in the fight against the British.

Buchanan and about two dozen men from the Lancaster area formed a company and headed for Baltimore, Maryland, the most likely target for the next British assault. The officer in charge sent them on a mission to take horses for the troops from neighboring farms. A few days later, Baltimore's defenders at Fort McHenry drove off the British, an event that led a local attorney, Francis Scott Key, to write a poem that was later called "The Star Spangled Banner." The words were set to music and became the U.S. national anthem.

# ENTERING POLITICS

After the British defeat, Buchanan and the other Lancaster volunteers returned home. Buchanan now focused on a new interest—politics. The same day the British burned Washington, Buchanan had accepted the nomination from the Federalist Party to run for a seat in the Pennsylvania House of Representatives.

The House, along with the Senate, formed the General Assembly, which proposed laws for the state. Across Pennsylvania, Democratic Republicans outnumbered Federalists, but the Federalists usually did well in Lancaster. When the election came in October 1814, Buchanan won his seat. At twenty-three, he became the youngest member of the General Assembly.

*Bombs and rockets explode over Fort McHenry during the unsuccessful British attack on Baltimore, September 13–14, 1814.*

James Buchanan Sr. had doubts about his son's interest in politics, preferring a focus on a law career. But the younger Buchanan believed the contacts he made in Harrisburg, the new state capital, would help him as a lawyer. The assembly members met for only three months of the year, so Buchanan would have plenty of time to practice law. His income quickly increased after his victory in the race for the House seat, proving the election's value to his law practice.

Over the next few years, Buchanan won attention for both his politics and his legal work. On July 4, 1815, he spoke to a group of Federalists about the recently completed War of 1812, which remained a topic of concern. Then and today, most experts thought that neither side had won a clear victory. The United States had neither gained nor lost land, and its capital was destroyed. But the Americans won several major battles, showing improved military skill as the war progressed. And the British released impressed American sailors and largely ended the practice thereafter. Perhaps most importantly for the Americans, the war boosted their pride. The financier Albert Gallatin, a government official at the time, thought the war made Americans "feel & act more as a Nation, and I hope that the permanency of the Union is thereby better secured."

Buchanan, though, thought Madison and the Jeffersonians had mismanaged the government badly and held that launching a war against Great Britain had been a mistake. The country had been unprepared to fight, and the Democratic Republicans refused to raise taxes to pay for the war effort. "Without money in the treasury," Buchanan said in his Fourth of July speech, "they rashly plunged us into a war with a nation more able to do us injury than any other in the world." Such views remained popular in Lancaster, and Buchanan was reelected to his seat in the fall of 1815.

## LIFE IN LANCASTER

Buchanan left the assembly in 1816, without completing his term, and concentrated on his law practice. His greatest fame came when he successfully defended a local judge during three **impeachment** trials. His success led to more legal business and rapidly increasing fees.

Buchanan also took time for leisure activities. He joined the Masons, a social organization dating back to the early eighteenth century that still exists today. In 1816 he ran an important local dance. And in 1818 he began dating a pretty young woman, Ann Coleman. Her father had made a fortune in iron and was one of the richest men in the country.

By this time, Buchanan was 6 feet tall and considered handsome. He had an odd habit of turning the left side of his head toward people when he spoke, giving the impression he was deeply interested in what they had to say. Actually, he was trying to overcome a problem that affected his eyesight. Ann, though, seemed to enjoy the impression that Buchanan was hanging on her every word. In 1819, having dated for a time, the couple became engaged. Ann broke the engagement, however, and just a few days afterward, she died. Buchanan later said she was the only woman he ever truly loved. Despite his loss, Buchanan remained focused on his career. He was ready to take on new political challenges.

## An Unfortunate End

The Ann Coleman–James Buchanan romance may have been doomed from the start. Some people whispered that the ambitious young lawyer was only after the woman's family's money. The Colemans may have believed this, since they seemed to have wanted their daughter to end the engagement. And Ann may have had some emotional problems. As her relationship with Buchanan progressed, Ann faulted him for not paying enough attention to her. The last straw was a rumor, heard by Ann, that Buchanan had spent time with another woman.

Buchanan did not show much emotion when his fiancée broke the engagement; he simply carried on with his business. But Ann's death did upset him, as did the rumors that swirled around when it became known that Ann had died of what doctors called "hysterical convulsions." This verdict suggested to some a physical fit resulting from mental suffering. Other people in Lancaster said the young woman had killed herself, upset over the breakup with Buchanan. Ann's friends thought Buchanan had murdered her, in effect, because of his behavior before the engagement ended. Because of their strong negative feelings, the Colemans refused to let Buchanan attend the funeral. Although he courted other women later in life, Buchanan never married and was the country's only bachelor president.

# ENTERING THE
# NATIONAL SCENE

*Two*

*T*hrough 1819 James Buchanan and other Lancaster Federalists turned their attention to national politics. Slavery was becoming a heated issue in Congress. Although slavery had been legal in America since colonial days, some Northern states had already outlawed the practice or planned to ban it soon. At the same time, new states were joining the Union as settlers moved west into the lands that formed the **Louisiana Purchase**. Some of the settlers of these new western lands were slaveowners. They expected slavery to be legal when the territories in the Louisiana Purchase became states. Some Northern lawmakers, however, opposed the spread of slavery to those lands.

In 1818 settlers in the Missouri Territory applied for statehood. This sparked a debate in Congress over whether the new state should allow slavery. Many residents owned slaves and expected to be able to keep them, or to buy new ones in the future if they wished. The debate continued into 1819, with some Northern lawmakers calling for a gradual end to slavery in Missouri as a condition of statehood. Southern lawmakers generally opposed this plan, as well as all other proposals to limit the spread of slavery westward. The issue was partially based on principle—under the Constitution, slavery was legal, and the Southerners believed western settlers should not be denied their rights. Limiting the spread of slavery would also upset the balance in Congress between free and slave states. The Southerners feared that over time, lawmakers from the free states in the North and West would dominate Congress and undercut Southern interests. For example, the Northerners might seek further restrictions on slavery or try to end it altogether.

In November 1819, while still engaged to Ann Coleman, Buchanan met with other Lancaster Federalists to discuss the debate over Missouri. They wanted their local representative in Congress to oppose the admission of Missouri as a slave state.

Into 1820 Congress continued to debate the issue. Finally, Henry Clay of Kentucky helped draft what became known as the Missouri Compromise. Missouri and Maine would be allowed to join the Union simultaneously. Maine would be a free state, while Missouri would be allowed to have slavery. In the future, all new territories in the Louisiana Purchase above a given latitude would enter the Union as free states. Those below the line of the map

## SLAVERY IN AMERICA

The first African slaves reached North America during the early sixteenth century, traveling with Spanish explorers. Africans first came to England's American colonies in 1619. They and American Indians served as both slaves and indentured servants through the century. By the eighteenth century, however, blacks were more commonly held as slaves, and not many worked as indentured servants. Slavery was legal everywhere in the American colonies, but it played a larger role in the South. The climate and terrain there favored the growing of cash crops on a vast scale. The first was tobacco, followed by rice, sugar, indigo, and later, cotton. In some colonies, such as South Carolina, African slaves soon outnumbered free whites. The long history of slavery in the South and its importance to the regional economy led Southerners to defend it strongly during Buchanan's lifetime.

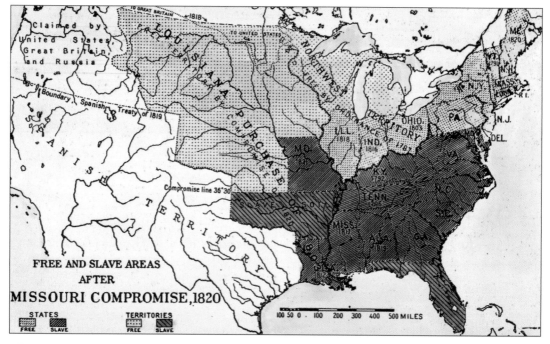

FREE AND SLAVE AREAS
AFTER
MISSOURI COMPROMISE, 1820

STATES          TERRITORIES
FREE  SLAVE     FREE  SLAVE

*This map of the United States shows the location of free and slave states and territories after the Missouri Compromise of 1820.*

described by "36 degrees, 30 minutes of latitude" (36°30') could allow slavery. The agreement, like most compromises, did not please everyone. But it ended the debate over slavery—for a time.

# THE NEXT POLITICAL STEP

In August 1820 the Federalists around Lancaster chose Buchanan as their candidate for the upcoming Congressional election. He actually represented the views of a new group in Pennsylvania calling themselves "Federalist Republicans." Democratic Republicans in the state were arguing with each other, and some left the party to work with the Federalists to try to win the state's governorship. On the national level, however, the Federalists remained weak and had virtually disappeared. The country had entered what is sometimes called the Era of Good Feelings. With James Monroe as president and a majority in Congress,

Democratic Republicans controlled both the executive and legislative branches of the United States.

The good feelings did not extend to Pennsylvania politics. Buchanan saw his opponents bring up the disastrous relationship with Ann Coleman and other personal issues, seeking to weaken his popular support. His father, seeing how angry his eldest son was, told the future president, "Let not your passions get the better of your sober judgment."

In most political campaigns of the day, candidates did not make many public appearances. Most let their supporters campaign for them, or wrote letters published in newspapers that supported their party. During his race for Congress, Buchanan spoke publicly only a few times and wrote no letters to newspaper editors. He preferred to remain behind the scenes and write directly to key leaders in the area. His strategy worked, and that fall he was elected to the U.S. House of Representatives.

The next session of Congress did not meet until the end of 1821, giving Buchanan additional time to pursue his legal career. Buchanan also had the unfortunate and unexpected task of sorting out his father's affairs. The senior Buchanan had received a fatal

*The U.S. Capitol was rebuilt after the British burned it in 1814. The building looked like this during most of Buchanan's years in Congress.*

head injury upon falling from a horse-drawn carriage. His son then had to make sure that Elizabeth Buchanan and the children still at home would have enough money to live.

## In Washington

Buchanan finally left for the nation's capital in November 1821. Washington, D.C., was still rebuilding after the devastating fire of 1814. Buchanan rented a room in a house with other representatives, a common arrangement at the time. He officially began his career in Congress on December 3 and was assigned to a committee that handled agricultural issues. Listening to some of the more experienced members speak, Buchanan expressed the opinion that "the reputation of many of them, stands higher than it deserves." Buchanan did well with his own speeches, and he became friendly with several important members of the House. One was William Lowndes of South Carolina. Lowndes was known for his speaking skills and was considered to be one of the wisest members of the House. In the years to come, Buchanan would forge more friendships in Washington that boosted his political career.

Buchanan ran for reelection in 1822 and won easily. By now the difference between the two national parties had blurred. Buchanan wrote that he saw "no trace of the old distinction between Federal and Democrat." Some Federalists now had Democratic beliefs, and even when Buchanan was serving in the Pennsylvania legislature, some Democrats had thought he should join their party. On certain issues he seemed closer to the Jeffersonians than to the Federalists.

The collapse of the old Federalist Party was soon complete. In the 1824 presidential election, four men calling themselves Democratic Republicans entered the race. Buchanan knew that to advance his own career, he would need the support of voters across Pennsylvania. He tried to measure which of the four presidential candidates was most popular back home. Some former Federalists were leaning toward Andrew Jackson, and Buchanan joined them.

Jackson had been one of the heroes of the War of 1812, winning the last U.S. victory of the war, the Battle of New Orleans. "Old Hickory," as he was known, also won fame fighting the Creek and Seminole Indians. Jackson's heroics made him popular, especially along the western frontier. People saw him as a simple man who supported the interests of farmers, just as Jefferson had. And, like Jefferson, he distrusted the power of a strong national government, thinking the states should have as much freedom as possible.

## BATTLE FOR THE PRESIDENCY

Jackson won the presidency, though in a controversial way. He claimed the most popular votes but did not win a majority in the **Electoral College**. Under the Constitution, the House of Representatives was then to choose the next president from among the top three candidates. With Jackson's strong support in Pennsylvania, Buchanan and the other representatives from the state seemed sure to vote for Old Hickory. But in the state and around the nation, some lawmakers feared that another candidate, Secretary of State John Quincy Adams, would make a deal with Speaker of the House Henry Clay to earn the powerful official's support, thus shutting out Jackson.

Although still a relatively unknown lawmaker, Buchanan threw himself into the controversy. He disliked Adams and wanted Clay to support Jackson. On December 30, Buchanan met with Jackson. He asked the general point-blank about a rumor going around: had Jackson made any kind of deal with Adams, offering him the job of secretary of state in return for Adams's support for the presidency? At the time, the post of secretary of state was regarded as a stepping-stone to the presidency, and Buchanan never wanted to see Adams in that office. Jackson refused to answer yes or no.

When the vote came in the House, Adams won the presidency, having gained Clay's support. He then named Clay his secretary of state, angering Jackson and his supporters. They believed rumors that Clay and Adams had made a "corrupt bargain—Clay's support for Adams in return for the top cabinet post.

During the next four years, President Adams struggled to deny the claim of a corrupt bargain. Even if he hadn't made a deal with Clay, many Americans believed he had, and Congress was reluctant to work with him. Across the country, Jackson's angry supporters said that Adams had stolen the election from Old Hickory, and they were already preparing for Jackson to run again.

Buchanan remained in Congress during those years, strengthening his ties to the Democratic Republicans (soon known simply as Democrats). In 1826 he began building a new Democratic-leaning party in Pennsylvania, and when he won reelection in 1828, he was openly calling himself a Democrat. He favored the party's support for states' rights, versus giving the federal government more power over the states.

Buchanan faced a minor political crisis in 1827. Rumors that he had somehow played a part in the corrupt bargain circulated. Jackson himself made the charge, and Buchanan denied it. He then angered Jackson by trying to defend himself in a letter to a Lancaster newspaper. He wrote, "I called upon General Jackson . . . solely as his friend . . . and not as the agent of Mr. Clay or any other person." Jackson and Buchanan remained political allies, but not friends. Buchanan learned he should keep his future political dealings and plans as quiet as possible. False rumors could ruin a political career.

# The Party Papers

Since the 1790s the U.S. political parties had counted on newspapers that supported their policies to praise them in print. The owners of the papers openly backed one party or the other and were often friendly with lawmakers and government officials. These "party papers" also violently attacked the opposing parties and their candidates. The party in power often helped its favored papers by giving them government printing jobs. Andrew Jackson's campaign of 1828 marked one of the low points in U.S. party journalism. The papers that backed Adams or Jackson published lies about the other candidate's personal affairs. Buchanan did not escape the attacks, either. A Pennsylvania paper that supported Adams falsely accused Buchanan of insulting the president's wife in public. Buchanan usually ignored the lies and distortion of the party papers. This time, however, he defended himself, vigorously denying the claim. As his political career advanced, Buchanan counted on papers that supported him to praise his policies and attack his political foes.

## The Age of Jackson

As the 1828 presidential campaign began, Buchanan once again supported Jackson while seeking his own reelection. Buchanan remained well liked in his district in Pennsylvania. He called for such popular measures as a tariff, or tax, on certain imported goods, so local goods would be cheaper, and money for improving roads. In the fall, both he and Jackson won their races, and Buchanan began thinking about his political future, hoping to soon run for the U.S. Senate.

Jackson's victory brought changes to American politics. The right to vote was expanded, and some politicians focused more on the common man than on wealthy investors. For Buchanan, protecting the rights of the states versus the federal government, a view he shared with a growing number of Southern friends in Congress, remained a major goal. One such friend was Senator William King of Alabama, a roommate of Buchanan's in the city. Most Southern lawmakers, even those who did not own slaves, supported the institution, and Buchanan shared their views. During a speech in 1830, he said that slavery was an evil, but he warned of the dangers if slavery were ever abolished, as former slaves would become masters over white men. "For my own part," he said, "I would, without hesitation . . . march . . . in defense" of the slave owners of the South."

By 1830 Buchanan was the head of the House Judiciary Committee, which addressed legal matters. He had shown his legal talents and devotion to the Constitution. But he had been disappointed when the Pennsylvania Democrats he worked with had not received important positions in the Jackson administration. His Democratic friends were also losing power back in Pennsylvania. Buchanan announced that he would retire from politics and not run again for Congress in 1832. But he still had one major role to play in Washington.

## MISSION TO RUSSIA

As Buchanan's days in Congress drew to a close, his political supporters in Pennsylvania were thinking about his future. In March 1831 Lancaster Democrats proposed that Buchanan be chosen as the party's vice presidential candidate in 1832. Others in the party suggested that Jackson should name him to his cabinet. The president, however, had other ideas.

Although Buchanan had supported Jackson, the Pennsylvanian's dispute with Jackson over the details of the corrupt bargain had turned Old Hickory against him. Jackson was known to call Buchanan names behind his back, once saying that he was an "inept busybody." But the call for Buchanan to run as vice president showed the president that the Pennsylvania congressman had supporters in the party. Jackson decided the best thing he could do was give Buchanan a government position that would keep him far from Washington. In May, he asked Buchanan to serve as the U.S. minister to Russia. In January 1832 the U.S. Senate approved the appointment, and in March Buchanan prepared to leave the United States for the first time in his life.

Buchanan had mixed emotions about his new position. In his diary he expressed sadness over leaving Lancaster for a long sojourn abroad. He wrote, "I was leaving a city where I had spent the best years of my life, where I had been uniformly a popular favorite, and, above all, where I had many good and true friends who had never abandoned me."

In St. Petersburg, the Russian capital at the time, Buchanan found a city filled with art and culture, and his home was equipped with fine silverware, china, and decorations. As a minister, he would be expected to entertain other diplomats in an impressive style. His main mission was to work out two treaties with the Russians—one to improve trade relations and one regarding legal rights at sea.

Over several months, Buchanan discussed the trade treaty with Russian diplomats, reaching a final agreement in December 1832. Among other things, the agreement guaranteed that U.S. merchant ships and their goods would receive the same treatment in Russian ports as they did at home. No other country had won the trading rights Buchanan secured for the United States.

*This engraving of Buchanan was based on a photo taken by Matthew Brady, who later became famous for his photography of the Civil War.*

Buchanan had less luck, however, with the second treaty dealing with rights at sea. He left St. Petersburg in August 1833 without an agreement. Several months before, he had learned that his mother was ill, and President Jackson had given him permission to return to the United States. Elizabeth Buchanan died, however, before her son could reach her bedside. Still, Buchanan was ready to come home.

With his diplomatic mission largely a success, Buchanan once again thought about his political career. In July he had written to a friend, "I think it more than probable that my political life is drawing to a close, and I confess I look upon the prospect without regret. [Political] office is not necessary for my happiness." But Buchanan knew he still had supporters in Pennsylvania who hoped to send him back to Congress, this time as a U.S. senator. And despite feelings he sometimes expressed, Buchanan was ready to serve again, too.

# DIVISION AND EXPANSION

## Three

*B*uchanan arrived in Philadelphia on November 24, 1833, greeted by friends who had already planned a lavish dinner in his honor. The state's lawmakers were just about to choose the next U.S. senator for Pennsylvania. At the time, senators were elected by the legislatures of each state, instead of by voters. Buchanan's friends hoped he would win the seat, but his long absence hurt his chances. And Buchanan, at President Jackson's request, did not campaign hard for the spot. The president did not want to upset the governor of Pennsylvania, who favored another candidate. Jackson assured Buchanan that he would get presidential support when the next Senate seat became available. Jackson already planned to name another Pennsylvania senator to fill Buchanan's old job as minister in Russia. Once that had come to pass, the way would be clear for Buchanan to go to the Senate.

## CONFLICTS AT HOME

During Buchanan's stay in Russia, the United States had faced two divisive issues. One involved the Bank of the United States. Alexander Hamilton had argued for its creation in 1791, believing that the country needed a strong national bank to help boost commerce. From the first, a wide range of people opposed the bank. Some disliked the fact that British investors owned stock in the bank. Others believed it competed against and harmed state banks. Jeffersonian Democrats opposed the bank because they saw it as another example of the Federalists favoring wealthy merchants and investors over farmers. These foes united in 1811 to prevent Congress from renewing the **charter** of the Bank of the United States.

Despite the opposition, the Second Bank of the United States was chartered in 1816. Jackson, who opposed the bank, vetoed a law that would have renewed its charter in 1836. This act started the "Bank War" between Jackson and the bank's supporters. The next year, Jackson took the government's funds out of the bank and put them in state banks.

In private, Buchanan had spoken in favor of the bank, but back in the United States, he followed the Democratic Party line and took Jackson's position. Buchanan once called the bank "dangerous to the rights and liberties of the people of the Union." Over the next few years, Buchanan remained a strong opponent of the bank, and its charter was never renewed.

The second explosive issue of the day involved an 1828 tariff law, but it soon grew to touch on a much larger issue. Congress hoped to increase manufacturing in the United States by taxing, or placing a tariff on, some imported industrial goods. What was good for the manufacturers, however, was bad for Southern farmers, particularly in South Carolina. The amount of cotton produced in the state was falling, as overfarming was draining the soil of nutrients. At the same time, prices for cotton were also declining. The farmers made less money and could not afford to buy the foreign goods they wanted. Attacking the tariff was one way to fight back.

In November 1832 South Carolina's lawmakers issued a statement saying that their state had the right to **nullify** a federal law if South Carolinians believed it violated the Constitution. Their position was that the states, not the Supreme Court, had the ultimate power to decide if a federal law was valid.

John C. Calhoun, Jackson's vice president, was from South Carolina, and he gave up his position, preferring to return to the Senate so that he could argue for this extreme view of states' rights. Calhoun took his state's position on nullification one step farther, saying that South Carolina had the right to secede if Jackson tried to enforce the tariff in the state.

Underneath the South Carolinians' anger about the tariff was another concern. The state relied on slavery to a huge extent. Since the days of the Missouri Compromise, abolitionists had been speaking and writing against slavery. Calling for the right to nullify federal laws was South Carolina's first step in making sure it could protect slavery from any future attacks by the federal government.

In 1833 Jackson responded to the nullification crisis by supporting a lower tariff. But he flatly rejected the notion of nullification itself, calling it "incompatible with the existence of the Union" and "inconsistent with every principle on which [the Constitution] was founded." Buchanan shared the president's views on nullification. But he was less sure whether secession could be allowed. Still, he feared what would happen to the country if a state did try to secede. Secession, especially over slavery, would most likely split the United States apart.

# BACK TO WASHINGTON

By the end of 1834 Jackson had kept his promise to open up a Senate seat in Pennsylvania, choosing Senator William Wilkins to take Buchanan's old job as minister to Russia. Pennsylvania's governor backed Buchanan for the empty seat and Buchanan returned to Washington, D.C., in December of that year. The Era of Good Feelings was now long over, and the Whig Party had

# Rise of Abolitionism

While James Buchanan was still at his diplomatic post in Russia, Great Britain took a major step in the advancement of human rights, abolishing slavery in August 1833. Abolitionism was on the rise in the United States too, as some opponents of slavery became more outspoken in their demand for immediate **emancipation** across the United States. The movement attracted free blacks and women, two social groups shut out of politics and positions of power at the time. William Lloyd Garrison helped organized the American Anti-Slavery Society in 1832 and was considered the leading abolitionist. Other key members were Lucretia Mott and the Grimké sisters of South Carolina. Most abolitionists based their views on religion, seeing slavery as a sin. They also believed slavery conflicted with the values of freedom and liberty held so dear in the United States. Most abolitionist groups did not have many members, and most people who opposed slavery called for its gradual end, not its immediate abolition. The extreme views of the abolitionists stirred some proslavery forces to violence. Still, the abolitionists remained dedicated to their ideas, which slowly began to sway some Northern public opinion against slavery. Buchanan did not like the early abolitionists, believing they wanted to spark deadly slave rebellions. He called the more extreme abolitionists "desperate fanatics" and "ignorant enthusiasts" who would cause great harm to the nation.

emerged as the major challenge to the Democrats. Its leaders in the Senate included Henry Clay and Daniel Webster, who was known for his speaking talents. The Whigs had some connections to the old Federalists, generally favoring commerce and the creation of a strong national government. Their main concern, though, was opposition to Jackson, because of his war against the Bank of the United States. Unlike the Federalists at their end, the Whigs were not centered in the Northeast. And the Democrats had support beyond the South. Both were truly national parties.

In the Senate, Buchanan once again served on the Judiciary Committee. He also took time to rebuild his support in Pennsylvania. He would need that backing if he sought even higher office, such as vice president or president. Buchanan also had to turn his attention to slavery, which was continuing to grow as a national issue.

In 1836 Senator Calhoun wanted to deny citizens the right to prevent **petitions** that called for limits on slavery in Washington, D.C. Buchanan was always ready to defend a Southerner's right to own slaves, but he quickly attacked Calhoun's position. Buchanan made clear his support for slavery as a constitutional right and his hatred of abolitionists. But on the right to petition, he said, "No government possessing any of the elements of liberty has ever existed, or can ever exist, unless its citizens or subjects enjoy this right." The Constitution guaranteed Americans the right to present their views to their lawmakers through petitions. Buchanan said that right must be protected.

Also in 1836 Buchanan won a full six-year term as a senator from Pennsylvania. He was eager to be secretary of state and was disappointed that the newly elected president, Martin Van Buren, did not choose him for any cabinet job. But Buchanan would continue to play a role in foreign affairs, as he was picked to head the Senate Foreign Relations Committee.

# POLITICAL AND PERSONAL AFFAIRS

Through 1837 America's lawmakers continued to debate the need for a national bank. The president of the Bank of the United States was able to get a charter to operate in Pennsylvania, making the issue a local one for Buchanan and the state's voters. In Lancaster and elsewhere citizens sometimes argued over the bank. The arguments came as the economy had taken a severe hit. The Panic of 1837, which has also been called an economic depression, resulted from many factors, including a cutback in British investments in the United States.

Buchanan, with his business expertise and skill with numbers, suggested the creation of a new federal agency to handle

*A cartoon attacking the policies of Andrew Jackson and the Democrats shows the hard times caused by the Panic of 1837. Workers don't have jobs, and hungry people line up to receive free bread.*

the distribution and collection of money. He did not want to call it a bank, since the Bank War had so divided the country. Van Buren borrowed many of his ideas and called the new agency the Sub-Treasury. In September 1837 Buchanan gave one of his most important speeches in Congress, supporting the Sub-Treasury. In Pennsylvania, though, his Whig opponents in the General Assembly called on him to vote against the bill that would create the new agency. Buchanan was supposed to follow the lawmakers' instructions, but he did not want to go against Van Buren. Buchanan managed to have the bill tabled, or not brought to a vote. He used his lawyerly skill to avoid taking a stand that would have hurt him politically.

Over the next several years, Buchanan fought several political battles in Pennsylvania. He sought to ensure that his

## SLAVES IN THE FAMILY

The Buchanan family never directly owned slaves, though an uncle of Buchanan's father had been a slaveowner when James Buchanan Sr. arrived in America. Slavery became more personal for Buchanan during the 1830s, when his sister Harriet married a Virginian whose family owned two slaves. Buchanan arranged to buy the slaves and free first one, then the other. One historian says this reflected Buchanan's personal hatred of slavery, even though he supported the constitutional right to own slaves. Others say that Buchanan was thinking in political terms. He preferred to arrange for the slaves' freedom rather than risk having his enemies make an issue of his sister's in-laws' slaves.

Democratic allies remained in power. He also faced several family crises. Two of his sisters died, and he became responsible for their estates. He also took care of a newly motherless nephew, whose father had died earlier. In the same period, Buchanan found time to date Mary Kittera Snyder, the niece of a Philadelphia friend. Although at one point Buchanan seems to have wanted to marry Snyder, in the end his family opposed the match and the couple broke off their relationship. Several years later, Buchanan had another serious relationship with a much younger woman, but the difference in ages led him to end it.

At the end of 1839 President Van Buren offered Buchanan a new position: attorney general of the United States. In that role, Buchanan would advise the president on legal matters. Buchanan, though, thought his career would suffer if he took what most people considered an unimportant cabinet position. He remained in the Senate, though he faced political difficulties there, too. In 1840 his political opponents began taunting him with the nickname "Ten Cent Jimmy." His Sub-Treasury, they claimed, would have lowered an average worker's wage to ten cents per day. The charge was not true, but some believed it and turned against Buchanan. Still, Buchanan had enough support in the legislature to win reelection to the Senate. And he was still thinking ahead, to a possible run for the presidency.

## LOOKING BEYOND THE BORDERS

While personal affairs and state politics took much of Buchanan's time, he also focused on the world outside the United States. On the Senate Foreign Relations Committee, he addressed laws and treaties dealing with foreign affairs. Buchanan thought the country was bound to one day extend from the Atlantic to the Pacific

## Manifest Destiny

Buchanan's views on the U.S. "mission" to expand across the continent—and perhaps beyond—were shared by other Americans of the day. After Buchanan made his speech citing American expansion as "a great and glorious mission," a New York newspaper editor used the term "Manifest Destiny" to describe this supposedly God-given task. Manifest Destiny was not a specific policy, but a set of beliefs that backed the actions of some U.S. presidents during the nineteenth century. Buchanan and others truly thought God wanted Americans to spread democracy and Protestant denominations to regions where they did not exist. This expansion could come peacefully, by buying land from other countries. At times, though, some Americans were ready to fight to claim what they thought they deserved. Some believers in Manifest Destiny simply wanted to show America's greatness to the world. Many slaveowners, however, saw expansion as a way to strengthen slavery. They assumed slavery would be allowed in some of these new lands, and the states formed from them would send proslavery lawmakers to Congress.

oceans, which would mean buying or taking lands then controlled by Mexico and Great Britain. He later said that Americans had "a great and glorious mission to perform . . . that of extending the blessings of Christianity and of civil and religious liberty over the whole North American continent. . . . We must fulfill our destiny."

Americans had already headed west. Before 1836 Texas was part of Mexico. That year, American settlers there, along with like-minded Mexicans, won a war for independence. Buchanan backed the Texas rebels and eventually supported a plan to **annex** Texas and make it part of the United States. Many lawmakers opposed annexation. Slavery was legal in Texas, and most representatives of free states did not want a new slave state in the Union. As he would in the future, however, Buchanan sided with Southerners on this issue.

Buchanan also supported acquiring land in what would be the future state of Oregon, where the Americans and British were arguing over the boundary. Buchanan believed it should be set at latitude 54 degrees and 40 minutes (54°40'). The dispute led some Democrats who favored expansion to cry, "Fifty-four, forty or fight!"; they were ready to go to war with Great Britain to get the land.

## Secretary of State

The threat of war with either Great Britain or Mexico seemed real as Americans prepared for the presidential election of 1844. Buchanan had been seeking the Democratic nomination for several years, but he saw that he did not have enough support and took himself out of the race. The party chose James K. Polk as its candidate, and he won the election. Buchanan had campaigned hard for the party ticket, and Polk rewarded his support by naming him secretary of state. Buchanan later said he would rather have used his legal skills on the Supreme Court. But his diplomatic expertise and knowledge of foreign affairs made him an able head of the State Department.

Settling the Oregon issue was one of Buchanan's first concerns. At Polk's direction, the United States accepted 49 degrees of latitude as the border in Oregon. Then, Polk and Buchanan turned their attention south. The United States annexed Texas in March 1845, angering the Mexicans and setting off a border dispute.

Mexico argued that Texas had much less land than it claimed. As a devout expansionist, President Polk supported the Texans. Polk sent U.S. troops to the border region, and in April 1846 fighting between those soldiers and Mexican troops led to the Mexican War.

Within two years, the United States had defeated Mexico. Buchanan led the call to take as much Mexican territory as possible. He and Polk argued over how much land to take. In the end, Buchanan lost, though the country still gained California and other lands west of Texas.

Throughout his service in the Polk administration, Buchanan clashed with the president over issues. Polk did not particularly like his secretary of state, once writing that Buchanan "has been selfish, and all his acts and opinions seem to have been controlled with a view to his own advancement, so much so that

*In September 1846, General Zachary Taylor led U.S. troops as they captured the city of Monterrey, Mexico.*

I can have no confidence or reliance on any advice he may give upon public questions." Other politicians shared Polk's thoughts. No one doubted that Buchanan was intelligent and a skilled politician. But his peers did not always trust him. He seemed to make decisions and take positions based on what was likely to help his career.

Despite any personal differences, Buchanan remained in the Polk cabinet through the president's one term. In 1848 Buchanan once again tried to win support for the Democratic presidential nomination but once again failed. The next year, he left Washington and moved back to Pennsylvania, taking up residence at Wheatland, a new estate he had bought in Lancaster. He was not actively serving in government, but politics and the issues of the day remained on his mind.

*Buchanan bought the 22-acre Wheatland Estate in 1848. It was named for the wheat fields that once covered the grounds.*

# DIFFICULT PATH TO THE PRESIDENCY

## Four

James Buchanan was fifty-eight years old when he settled in at Wheatland. He had already served in government for thirty-five years, earning the nickname "Old Public **Functionary**" from his political critics. They thought he had taken many government jobs but had not done much that was important. His supporters sometimes referred to him as "Old Buck." The long years of political battle might have made some men ready for retirement. But Buchanan loved the political arena and truly cared about the issues the country faced. Slavery was again at the top of the list.

*During his career, Buchanan enjoyed a comfortable lifestyle. He amassed a fortune worth about $5 million in current dollars.*

## THE COMPROMISE OF 1850

The U.S. victory over Mexico gave the federal government almost 500,000 square miles of new territory. The true prize was California, where gold had been discovered in 1848. The next year, Californians asked to join the Union as a free state, setting off angry debates in Congress.

President Zachary Taylor had suggested that New Mexico also join the Union as a free state, which upset the supporters of slavery, who had assumed that some of the new lands in the West would become slave states. The Missouri Compromise of 1820 had outlawed slavery in the Louisiana Purchase above latitude 36 degrees and 30 minutes. The Southerners suggested extending the line out to the Pacific Ocean, thus permitting slavery in new lands below the line. That change, though, would have allowed slavery in part of California, and the country's growing antislavery forces resisted any effort to spread slavery westward. Some Southerners, for their part, proposed drastic action if the northern Whigs and a new political party, the Free Soilers, tried to limit the expansion of slavery. The Southerners' solution: disunion, or splitting the nation in two, one half slave and one half free.

As in 1820, Henry Clay stepped in to offer a compromise. After weeks of debate over his plan and other ideas, Congress passed the Compromise of 1850. California entered the Union as

*Henry Clay (center), helped push the Compromise of 1850 through Congress, temporarily delaying more arguments over the spread of slavery.*

*Slave catchers, often armed, traveled to the North to find and return runaway slaves to their masters.*

a free state, while New Mexico and Utah became territories. The residents of the territories would decide for themselves whether to allow slavery or not to allow it, a concept called popular sovereignty. Also as part of the compromise, Congress passed a new fugitive slave law, requiring free states to help in the capture and return of runaway slaves. The slave trade was abolished in Washington, D.C., but slavery remained legal in the nation's capital.

Increasingly, opposition to the new compromise came from certain lawmakers from the North and the South who had extreme views on slavery—for or against. But members of both parties with more moderate views saw the plan as the best way to save the Union. Buchanan had split feelings. He remained committed to defending the rights of slaveowners to bring their human property into new territories. He also called for extending the Missouri Compromise line to the Pacific. But he favored the tougher fugitive slave law that emerged from the compromise.

## FUGITIVE SLAVES IN PENNSYLVANIA

Even before 1850, Northerners were expected to help return fugitive slaves to their owners, but many ignored the law. The new Fugitive Slave Act gave the federal government and slaveowners more power to go into free states and track down runaways. Buchanan believed Northerners had a legal duty to cooperate with individuals and government agents acting in compliance with the law. In the process, they would also show proslavery forces that the North was not focused on destroying slavery. But an 1851 incident in Buchanan's own Lancaster County showed how unpopular the new law was in the North. In the village of Christiana, a group of free blacks and a few whites armed themselves to try to stop the removal of a runaway slave. The protesters killed the slaveowner and hurt several other people. Soon newspapers were writing about the "Christiana riot." To Southerners, it was a sign of the growing Northern extremism against both the laws and slavery. To abolitionists, defending the runaway slave was seen as a heroic, moral act. That difference of opinion over slavery would continue to deepen, much to Buchanan's disappointment.

Thus Buchanan wanted to preserve the Union, but he saw forces at work that threatened to pull it apart. Popular sovereignty would pose problems, as opposing factions in a territory would clash over whether slavery should be allowed. The whole issue, Buchanan wrote a friend, made him think, "that in four years from this time the union will not be in existence as it now exists.

There will be two Republics." Clearly, Buchanan saw disunion as a likely result of the growing arguments over slavery.

## MORE POLITICS AND DIPLOMACY

The country's slavery issue did not deter Buchanan from once again seeking the Democratic Party's nomination for president in 1852. In Pennsylvania, though, he had lost some support from lawmakers who thought he too often sided with the South on slavery. Buchanan, and other Northerners like him, were called "doughfaces." Their views were said to be easy to shape and change, like dough. The nickname was particularly aimed at Northern lawmakers who supported Southern views on slavery.

Buchanan lost the nomination to Franklin Pierce, another Northern doughface. Buchanan said his political career was over: "After a long and stormy public life, I shall go into retirement without regret." But President Pierce quickly changed that plan by asking Buchanan to serve as the U.S. minister to England. As with President Jackson and the mission to Russia decades before, Buchanan sensed Pierce merely wanted to get rid of him. Use his skills, yes, but also keep him out of politics so Buchanan would not be a favored candidate for president in 1856. Even so, Buchanan took the job.

In 1855 the United States and England were arguing over affairs in the Caribbean and Central America. Both countries were interested in acquiring Cuba. Both hoped to someday dig a canal across Central America, to link the Atlantic and Pacific oceans. In London Buchanan tried to smooth out the problems in the region.

The Americans wanted the British to leave part of Nicaragua's coast they had occupied, arguing that the British presence there violated an earlier treaty. The British were also on several islands off the broad northern coast of Honduras. Buchanan stressed the American view: the British should leave both areas. The British refused. The two sides talked for more than two years without agreement. The British eventually sent more ships to the region, to show their plans to stay.

During his tour in London, Buchanan had better luck with helping to extend U.S. fishing rights in Canada. He also worked on the Ostend Manifesto, named for the Belgian town where it was written. The report spelled out American intentions regarding Cuba. The United States hoped to buy the island, but it declared the right to take Cuba if the Spanish refused. The Spanish had not protected Americans living in Cuba, and the only way the U.S. government could keep its citizens safe was

## CLOTHES MAKE THE DIPLOMAT

Soon after he arrived in London, James Buchanan created a stir because of his wardrobe. Foreign ambassadors and ministers were expected to dress formally at government events. But the U.S. State Department had asked Buchanan and others to avoid fancy clothes and to appear "in the simple dress of an American citizen." Buchanan supported this rule, but he also knew that the British would be offended if he ignored their expectations. The minister decided to compromise: he wore simple clothes, along with a sword. The sword satisfied the English, while in America, a local newspaper and several friends applauded him for not giving in totally to the English bias.

to control the island. The Ostend Manifesto reflected Buchanan's desire to expand the Union. And since slavery was legal in Cuba, its admission would bring a new slave state, an idea Southerners cheered.

## BLEEDING KANSAS AND PRESIDENTIAL POLITICS

Buchanan returned to America in April 1856. He had already received the good news that the Democrats in Pennsylvania planned to support him at the upcoming Democratic convention. At the convention, the party would choose its candidate for president. As in the past, Buchanan did not say much publicly about running for president, but most Democrats knew he still wanted the office.

During Buchanan's absence, the slavery debate had turned from words to violence. In 1854 Congress passed the Kansas-Nebraska Act, which created two new territories out of the Louisiana Purchase. Both Kansas and Nebraska sat above the 36°30' line and should have been free. But to gain support for the bill in the South, Senator Stephen A. Douglas called for overturning the Missouri Compromise of 1820. He said the settlers should be the ones to decide whether to allow slavery—popular sovereignty. Kansas, which lay next to the slave state of Missouri, would presumably also allow slavery. Nebraska, farther north and bordering free states, would most likely become a free state.

In response to the Kansas-Nebraska Act, extreme antislavery forces from the North began sending settlers to Kansas. They wanted to make sure the government there was shaped by abolitionist views. In response, some slaveowners in neighboring Missouri crossed the border to cast illegal ballots in Kansas

In 1856 Missourians stream into Kansas, intent on installing a proslavery government in the territory.

elections. They wanted to create a proslavery government in the new territory. By the end of 1855, Missourians and Northerners in Kansas were sometimes raiding each other's towns as they battled to control the territory. The violence increased in 1856, when abolitionist John Brown and his sons killed five proslavery Kansans, retaliating for an earlier raid. The territory was now called "Bleeding Kansas."

Bleeding Kansas and popular sovereignty dominated the 1856 presidential campaign. In June, just several weeks after the Brown murders, the Democrats chose Buchanan as their candidate for president. He pledged to defend the party platform. It included, among other things, a commitment to popular sovereignty and "non-interference by Congress with slavery in state and territory, or in the District of Columbia." Buchanan saw popular sovereignty as part of the principle of self-government Americans cherished. Slavery, he said, had "too long distracted and divided the people of this Union," but he believed the Kansas-Nebraska Act would eventually "allay [ease] the dangerous excitement."

Buchanan's views, however, did not seem realistic. Several weeks before, Senator Charles Sumner of Massachusetts, after

# RISE OF THE REPUBLICANS

The Kansas-Nebraska Act led to the crumbling of one national political party and the creation of a new one. Northern Whigs mostly opposed the act, while Southern Whigs favored it. Some of the Southerners began moving into Democratic Party, which also largely favored popular sovereignty and the end of the Missouri Compromise. The Northern Whigs and some antislavery Northern Democrats then joined forces with the Free Soilers. The small Free Soil Party, formed during the 1840s, opposed the spread of slavery. Together, these forces created the Republican Party, which held its first official meeting in July 1854 in Jackson, Michigan. The party was not connected to the old Jeffersonian Republicans. Over the next few years, the Republicans also gained members from the American, or "Know-Nothing," Party. This party had originally formed to protect the rights of working Americans and to protest the immigration of Irish Catholics. By 1860 some Northern Know-Nothings saw slavery, not immigration, as the country's most important issue.

speaking out strongly against the South and slavery, had been viciously attacked in Congress by a Southern lawmaker. Emotions were higher than ever across the country, with some Southerners calling for secession if Republican John C. Frémont won the presidency. Buchanan himself feared a Republican win would mean disunion, as some Republicans, such as New York governor William H. Seward and Speaker of the House Nathaniel P. Banks, either called for a war against slavery or

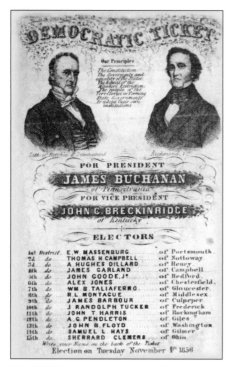

An 1856 campaign poster advertises Buchanan as the Democratic candidate for president and John C. Breckinridge as his running mate for vice president.

disunion, if slavery were not abolished. Also running was former president Millard Fillmore, of the American Party. Like Buchanan, Fillmore campaigned on a platform of preservation of the Union.

## Victory

Despite the strong feelings, Buchanan struck many Americans as a good choice for president. He favored both preserving the Union and the right to slavery. He had experience as both a lawmaker and a diplomat. Moreover, his time in England had kept him out of the political debates over Kansas. He was not closely tied to one side or the other in the argument.

When voters went to the polls in the fall of 1856, their choices reflected the split over slavery. In twelve states where slavery was legal, not one person voted for Frémont, and Buchanan took the majority of votes in those states. In the Electoral College, Buchanan swept the South and added several midwestern states, California, and his home state of Pennsylvania. With his victory, Buchanan thought the worst was over for the country. All the North had to do was "permit our Southern neighbors to manage their own domestic affairs." His goal, he wrote a friend, was to end Northern "agitation" over slavery and "destroy sectional parties."

*A photo taken toward the end of the Buchanan administration shows the president surrounded by his cabinet.*

Buchanan's first major task was to select his cabinet. Buchanan partly considered where the members lived. He needed someone from New England and would reward someone from his home state. He also wanted Southerners, to ease the fears in the region about new attacks on slavery. Most historians think, however, that the choices Buchanan made showed that he favored the concerns of the South. Several of the cabinet members owned or had owned hundreds of slaves. The Northerners he picked were considered doughfaces during their political careers. Buchanan ignored the concerns of the almost 1.5 million voters who had supported Frémont, and the many others who couldn't vote and supported Republican positions—women and free African Americans. With his choices, Buchanan created a cabinet that mostly thought as he did. Its members would not be likely to challenge him or his decisions.

# DRED SCOTT

*Dred Scott first sued for his freedom in a Missouri court in 1846.*

Buchanan did not wait until his March 1857 inauguration to begin to advance his position on important issues. In February, the justices of the U.S. Supreme Court were about to decide an important case involving slavery. Dred Scott and his wife had brought their owner to court, seeking their freedom. They had traveled with the owner to a free state and a free territory, then returned to a slave state. Some Northern courts during the 1830s and 1840s said that a slave who spent time in a free state could sue for freedom. Scott's case reached the Supreme Court in 1856.

The Court's decision could settle several major issues. Did Congress have the right to outlaw slavery in territories? If it did, popular sovereignty would no longer apply. Were slaves citizens of the states where they lived or of the United States? If neither, they could not sue their owners, as the Scotts had done. Did the state laws regarding slaves brought within their borders apply? If not, then slaves could no longer sue for their freedom simply because their masters took them to live in free states.

The Court at the time had five Southerners, all Democrats, and four Northerners—two Democrats and two Republicans. The Southerners favored the arguments of slaveowners and slave states. The two Northern Democrats would influence what exactly the court allowed or outlawed in its decision in the Dred Scott case.

In early February, Buchanan wrote a letter to John Catron, one of the Southern justices and an old friend. Buchanan wanted to know if the Court would reach a decision before the inauguration in March. A few weeks later, Catron wrote back suggesting that Buchanan write Robert Grier, a Pennsylvania Democrat who also served on the Court. Grier was one of the two Northerners unsure of how to vote. Catron did

*Chief Justice Roger Taney delivered his decision in the* Dred Scott *case on March 6, 1858. It has often been called one of the worst decisions ever by the U.S. Supreme Court.*

not tell Buchanan what to say, but the president-elect knew what Catron meant. Buchanan should tell Grier about his hope for settling major issues regarding slavery, which the president-elect did not want to deal with, once in office. Buchanan did not have to say how he wanted Grier to vote. Both Catron and Buchanan believed that Grier would understand that the incoming president wanted legal protection for slavery in the territories.

At his inauguration, Buchanan exchanged a few words with Roger B. Taney, who was chief justice of the United States Supreme Court. No one knows what the two men said. But Buchanan already knew, through his contact with Grier, how the Court would rule on the *Dred Scott* case. That decision would please Buchanan and slaveowners. The president, however, did not tip his hand. In his inaugural address, he simply said, "to [the Supreme Court's] decision, in common with all good citizens, I shall cheerfully submit, whatever this may be."

Chief Justice Taney wrote the opinion for the Court, which appeared two days later. He said that slaves were not citizens but

*James Buchanan was sworn in as the fifteenth president on the steps of the U.S. Capitol. He gave his inaugural address from the same spot.*

merely property. Their owners could bring them wherever they chose, and the slaves had no legal right to sue for their freedom. Taney and six of the other justices also said that Congress could not outlaw slavery in a territory. In effect, the Taney Court was declaring that the Missouri Compromise of 1820 had violated the Constitution. The decision outraged Republicans. They remembered Buchanan and Taney exchanging words on March 4, and some wondered if Buchanan had been part of another "corrupt bargain" of some kind. The truth about Buchanan's role in the decision did not come out for years.

Buchanan ignored the Republican attacks. He thought they, not slavery, were the greatest danger to the country. And he gladly accepted the *Dred Scott* decision. He later said that it brought calm to the country. Few people, however, agreed with him.

For the most part, Southerners joined President Buchanan in welcoming the *Dred Scott* decision. But abolitionists and many opponents of slavery across the country detested it. So did free blacks, who saw their status threatened. Even whites who did not favor abolishing slavery thought the Court had gone too far. One of them was Abraham Lincoln, a leading Illinois Republican. Lincoln was preparing to run against Stephen Douglas in 1858 for Douglas's U.S. Senate seat. Lincoln said the Court ignored the fact that free blacks in some states could vote when the Constitution was ratified. Surely the country's founders recognized that these blacks had legal rights. Lincoln believed that the words of the Declaration of Independence meant what they said: all men are created equal. Lincoln did not extend this interpretation to support the position that in America blacks were entitled to equality with whites. Many Westerners who opposed the spread of slavery also held the same view. But Lincoln did believe that free blacks should have certain legal rights and that the spread of slavery should end.

## KANSAS AGAIN

The *Dred Scott* decision stirred strong opinions in Kansas, where pro- and antislavery forces were still fighting for control. The Court had said that Congress could not outlaw slavery there or in any other territory. Thus the people could decide for themselves what they wanted to do. Buchanan, who had supported the Kansas-Nebraska Act of 1854, was now ready to accept the people's will in Kansas on slavery. The issue, though, was not clear-cut.

When Buchanan took over the presidency, Kansas had two competing territorial governments. In 1855 Kansans had voted to choose legislators. Antislavery voters had refused to take part in the balloting because of fraud that gave the proslavery forces an unfair advantage. The election created a proslavery legislature that met in the territorial capital of Lecompton. The antislavery forces, sometimes called Free Staters, set up their own government in Topeka. Buchanan knew about the fraud that created the Lecompton government, but he believed he had to support the proslavery body and "protect it from the violence of lawless men, who were determined either to rule or ruin." Buchanan's desire to uphold the law put him in conflict—again—with the antislavery forces across the nation.

Buchanan named Robert Walker the governor of Kansas. He wanted Walker to arrange for Kansans to approve a new constitution that would take effect when the territory became a state. The major issue, of course, was whether Kansas would allow slavery. But with two governments and bitter feelings on both sides, resolution would not come easily. The importance of the issue went beyond Kansas and touched the whole country. One Georgian wrote to his U.S. senator, "If Kansas comes in as a free state, Buchanan will richly deserve death, and I hope some patriotic man will inflict it."

The Lecompton government held a convention in October 1857 to debate the future state constitution. During this time, Kansas had another election marred by rampant voter fraud. One proslavery region populated by only a handful of families recorded 1,200 votes. At the convention, the delegates drafted a constitution that allowed slavery, then said the voters would not have a chance to approve the document. Buchanan refused to accept that arrangement, believing that Kansans had a right to vote on the new constitution. Under pressure, the delegates agreed to let their fellow citizens vote on the issue of slavery, but not the entire constitution. The choice would be accept the new constitution with slavery, or accept it without. Buchanan approved of this, but Free State Kansans did not. The antislavery forces represented in Topeka greatly outnumbered the Lecompton supporters. But the opponents of slavery would not accept the Lecompton constitution and refused to vote. Not surprisingly, the proslavery forces voted to accept the constitution,

*Stephen Douglas served in Congress from 1843 until his death in 1861.*

hence to allow slavery. Free Staters later held their own vote and rejected the Lecompton constitution.

## THE LITTLE GIANT

Before and during his presidency, James Buchanan sometimes found himself opposing another popular Democrat, Stephen A. Douglas. The Illinois lawmaker was just 5 feet, 4 inches tall, but because of his powerful personality, he was known as "the Little Giant." Like Buchanan, Douglas started his career as a Northerner who opposed the abolitionists. And like the president, Douglas favored Western expansion. He wrote the Kansas-Nebraska Act, in part, to win Southern support for the creation of the Nebraska Territory. During the early 1850s, Buchanan rightly saw Douglas as a rival for the presidency. Douglas stepped aside for the presidency in 1856, thinking Buchanan would support him in the future. The two men, however, became political enemies over Kansas and Buchanan's strong support for Southern policies on slavery.

Some Northern members of the Democratic Party called on Buchanan to step in. The new constitution, which clearly did not represent the views of most Kansans, was tainted by all the fraud and divisions within Kansas. The Northern Democrats, led by Stephen A. Douglas, wanted Buchanan to call for a new convention. Douglas believed that if popular sovereignty meant anything, the people had to be given a real choice in a fair election. Buchanan rejected this argument. He also reminded Douglas that President Jackson had once destroyed the careers of fellow Democrats who challenged him. Douglas shot back, "Mr. President, I wish you to remember that General Jackson is dead." Douglas was not going to back down, though he could not do much to alter the situation in Kansas. Buchanan allowed the Lecompton constitution to go to Congress, which approved it in March 1858. Kansas voters, however, later rejected a proposal

## KING COTTON AND SLAVERY

In March 1858 South Carolina senator James Henry Hammond gave a speech supporting the Lecompton constitution of Kansas. He boasted that if the South ever seceded, it would be a powerful nation, blessed with natural resources and a strong economy. The reason for that strength was cotton, Hammond said: "Cotton is king." The invention of the cotton gin during the 1790s had made cotton a key Southern crop because it efficiently removed the seeds from the kind of cotton that grew across much of the region. The planting of more cotton led to the growth of slavery in the South, as farmers bought more slaves into lower southern states to raise the crop.

(continued)

By the 1850s almost all the cotton bought by Northern mills came from the South. This connection showed that even if the North abolished slavery, many factory owners and workers would continue to rely on the work of slaves for their profits. Cotton was also the main U.S. crop sold overseas, so sailors and shipowners also had ties to the slavery system that produced so much cotton. And anyone who bought clothes made of cotton was also helping the slave economy that thrived in the South. Hammond thought the slave economy, obviously good for white plantation owners, helped the slaves, too. At times in the North, there was not enough work for people who did not have skills or a good education. In the South, Hammond said, at least slaves were cared for by their masters. "There is no starving, no begging, no want for employment among our people. . . . Why, you meet more beggars in one day, in any single street of the city of New York, than you would meet in a lifetime in the whole South." Hammond's claim was not true, but by 1858, Southerners eager to defend slavery believed this and similar arguments.

PICKING.

that tied acceptance of the new constitution to a provision they did not favor. The territory still did not have a constitution that settled the slavery issue.

## OTHER CONCERNS

Kansas dominated Buchanan's first year in office, but it was not the only issue. The economy began to struggle late in 1856, when Great Britain cut back on the amount of grain purchased from U.S. farmers. The next year, the branch of a large American insurance company failed. During the summer, a ship carrying gold that belonged to the U.S. government sank and the gold was lost. Banks soon stopped lending money, companies fired workers, and a major depression began. That winter of 1857–1858, citizens in some Northern cities rioted, angry over the lack of work and food. The South, though, did not suffer as badly as the North. Foreign demand for cotton, its main crop, remained high.

In his first State of the Union address in 1857, Buchanan said the depression had one main cause—unwise investments in the stock market, fueled by banks that made dangerous loans. He noted "the suffering and distress prevailing among the people," adding, "with this the Government cannot fail deeply to sympathize, though it may be without the power to extend relief." The idea of the government widely spending money to help ease the pain of a severe economic downturn did not take root until the Great Depression of the 1930s.

During his term, Buchanan also dealt with a conflict even farther west than Kansas. During the 1840s, members of the Church of Jesus Christ of Latter-Day Saints, Mormons, had begun settling in Utah. They came under U.S. control when the government bought the land from Mexico in 1848 and created the territory of Utah.

By 1857 the Mormons were sometimes arguing with federal judges in Utah. The Mormons wanted to live independently under their leader, Brigham Young. Buchanan removed Young as the governor of the territory, appointed another one, and sent 2,500 troops to Utah to support the new governor. Young said he and his people would rather die than give up their local control. Both sides prepared to fight in the spring of 1858, but peace talks ended an all-out war.

*In 1846 Brigham Young led the Mormons from a settlement in Illinois to their new home in Utah.*

In foreign affairs, Buchanan remained committed to Manifest Destiny. He largely acted as his own secretary of state, drawing on his experience as a diplomat. He discussed buying Alaska from the Russians, though nothing came of that, and he continued to talk about buying Cuba. He held talks that led to a weakened British presence in Central America. This effort was part of his larger plan to promote greater U.S influence in the hemisphere. Buchanan also supported trade with China and Japan.

# Buchanan the President

Buchanan had entered the presidency as an experienced politician and lawmaker. With no wife and children, he had focused his adult life on his career. His friendships in Washington were important to him, and he spent a lot of time with his cabinet, both at work and outside the Executive Mansion, the presidential residence at 1600 Pennsylvania Avenue.

Some historians once claimed that Buchanan relied on his cabinet too much or took orders from them. The opposite was probably more correct. Several of these appointed officials were his friends, and they all shared similar views. If there was a disagreement, or if one cabinet member did something wrong, Buchanan quickly made a ruling or criticized the man who had erred. The members did not have to direct Buchanan, since during most of his presidency they shared the same goals: preserving the Union and slavery. Regarding the idea of Buchanan taking orders, cabinet member Jeremiah Black called him "a stubborn old gentleman, very fond of having his own way." The bigger problem, Black said, was that Buchanan sometimes was not sure what exactly he wanted to do.

Buchanan followed a precise schedule, working from 9 to 5 with an hour break. After an early dinner he usually worked several hours more before going to bed. When he wasn't working, Buchanan liked to visit with his friends and entertain guests. His

*U.S. troops on their way to Utah in 1857, before peace talks ended the threat of a full-scale war with the Mormons.*

# The First "First Lady"

Harriet Lane was the daughter of Buchanan's sister Jane. Harriet's parents died when she was a child, and her uncle took her into his home. "Nunc," as she called him, arranged for her schooling. By the time Buchanan won the presidency, Harriet was a well-educated, popular young woman. She had traveled with "Nunc" when he served as U.S minister to Great Britain, and at the Executive Mansion she was called the First Lady. After her, this title was applied to the wife of the sitting president. Harriet arranged parties, where she served fine food and drink and arranged for musicians to play. The president, however, would not let his guests play cards or dance in his home. Harriet later married and remained an important figure in the social life in the capital.

niece Harriet Lane came with him to Washington, and she organized parties at the presidential mansion. Buchanan also liked to stroll along the streets of Washington. And he enjoyed restful vacations in Bedford Springs, Pennsylvania. But a president facing a divided nation did not have much time for rest.

# The Election of 1858

Buchanan was not seeking office in the off-year election of 1858, but he and his policies played an important role in the campaign. Stephen Douglas, hoping to keep his Senate seat, made the Lecompton constitution and popular sovereignty two of the key issues. In Congress, he had spoken harshly against the proslavery constitution for Kansas. Buchanan blamed Douglas for stirring up antislavery feelings in the South and for not accepting the Dred Scott decision as the final word on slavery in the territories. The Democrats now seemed close to splitting along North-South lines, as the Whigs had done several years before.

The difference between the two powerful Democrats was not just political. Buchanan and Douglas did not like each other. Some Buchanan supporters thought the president's anger over Douglas could make their friend sick. Douglas did not directly attack Buchanan with words, but he refused to change his stance to suit the president. He told one senator, "I do not recognize the right of anybody to expel me from the Democratic Party!"

President Buchanan hated the Republican Party and feared that if it gained power, it would destroy the nation. By now, Democrats often referred to the opposing party's members as "Black Republicans," a racist tag that stressed their ties to African Americans. Still, as much as Buchanan worried about the Republicans, he hoped Douglas would lose his Senate race. The administration tried to convince Democrats in Illinois to desert Douglas, and it arranged for the firing of pro-Douglas Democrats in the state who held government jobs. Buchanan offered to stop those acts if Douglas would stop attacking the president and his policies. Douglas, though, believed he had to criticize the Lecompton constitution to keep his seat. Many Illinois voters opposed

Kansas's becoming a slave state. The political war with Buchanan dragged on.

Douglas's campaign and his views on Kansas soon became the focus of national attention. In August 1858, he and Abraham Lincoln began a series of seven debates across Illinois. Lincoln was the Republican candidate for Douglas's seat. Thousands of people came to hear them, and newspapers across the country reported what they said.

Throughout the debates, Lincoln asserted his belief that slavery should

*During their famous debates, Stephen Douglas and Abraham Lincoln spoke for hours at a time, with the crowds cheering for the candidate they supported.*

not be allowed in any territories. Unlike Douglas, he did not favor popular sovereignty. Douglas accused Lincoln and the Republicans of being secret abolitionists, no matter what they said in public. Lincoln gladly pointed out the feud between Douglas and Buchanan, showing how the party was splitting apart. Douglas tried to show where he and Buchanan shared the same views. In the end, Douglas was chosen by the state legislature. But Lincoln had actually won more popular votes and national fame. The Republicans were gaining strength as a political party in the North. Buchanan called the Democrats' losses in the election "so great that it is almost absurd." The sectional divide of the Union that Buchanan feared was drawing closer.

*John Brown kneels by the side of his dying sons during the battle at the Harper's Ferry armory.*

# REBELLION IN VIRGINIA

In his annual speech to Congress in December 1858, Buchanan blamed all the problems in Kansas on the supporters of the Topeka government. He once again ignored the fraud that had led to the division in the territory. With Kansas and other issues, Buchanan did not tolerate people who chose to challenge laws or upset public order. He said in the same speech, "resistance to lawful authority under our form of government can not fail in the end to prove disastrous to its authors." The country would soon see an example of this.

In October 1859, the abolitionist John Brown, of "Bleeding Kansas" fame, put in motion another violent attack. Along with some white supporters and a few blacks, Brown tried to seize an **armory** in Harpers Ferry, Virginia (now West Virginia). The U.S. military soon arrived, killing most of the attackers. Brown and several others fled but were captured. By year's end, Brown had been hanged for the crime of treason.

John Brown's raid scared and angered most Southerners. To them, it was further proof that abolitionists would not rest until they ended slavery everywhere. Many Northerners rejected Brown's violent ways. Yet others accepted his argument that slavery was an evil that had to end sooner rather than later. Just before his execution, Brown predicted that only bloodshed would erase the "crime" of slavery. Buchanan hoped to prevent that bloodshed. But events were moving beyond his control.

As 1859 drew to a close, President Buchanan spoke about John Brown and his actions at Harpers Ferry. He called the raid on the armory "sad and bloody," and said it was "a solemn warning to us all to beware of the approach of danger." He called on both Northerners and Southerners to end "the demon spirit of sectional hatred and strife now alive in the land."

To many Americans, however, Buchanan's words had little value. Antislavery Northerners saw him repeatedly side with the South. He did not understand Republican anger over the attempts to extend slavery. Yet more Northerners now saw the evils of slavery, which denied African Americans their rights, broke up families, and often resulted in harsh living conditions and cruel beatings.

The growing effort to limit the expansion of slavery worried slaveholders. Southerners felt Black Republicans and abolitionists would keep trying to deny their legal right to own slaves. And slavery was not just a legal issue. Some Southerners turned to religion to support their views. Slavery had existed during ancient times, when the Bible was written. The holy book said masters should treat slaves well, but it never called for the abolition of the practice of slavery.

Some Southerners, called fire-eaters, held extreme views. They continued to talk about secession as the only way to preserve slavery. The upcoming presidential election, some people thought, would decide whether the Union would split apart or remain whole.

# Conflict in Government

During the first months of 1860, President Buchanan faced a problem within his own government. Republicans controlled Congress, and they decided to investigate possible corruption by members of the Buchanan administration. The president said Congress did not have the power to investigate the executive branch, an idea the lawmakers rejected. Republican John Covode of Pennsylvania led a committee that studied the corruption issue. He wanted to see if Buchanan and his cabinet had illegally tried to influence the 1859 vote on the Lecompton constitution. For several months, the Covode Committee questioned witnesses, who included some of Buchanan's political friends. Others were members of Congress. The committee learned that the administration had bribed lawmakers to support the Lecompton constitution. Other witnesses claimed that Buchanan used government money to support Democrats who backed him and opposed Stephen Douglas. One cabinet member sent workers from his department to Kansas and paid them to support Buchanan's policies there. Democrats saw the Covode Committee as a political attack on their party. Republicans, they charged, were looking to weaken the Democrats in the upcoming election. The Republicans did use the committee's report to argue that the Democrats could not be trusted. But the committee also found real evidence of corruption. Still, Covode did not think Buchanan could be impeached. Buchanan felt that since he was not impeached, he was innocent of any wrongdoing. But Republicans continued to believe that he had led one of the most corrupt administrations of the era, a view that is supported by some historians.

# A Bitter Race for President

Buchanan declined to seek reelection in 1860. But he had a strong interest in the future Democratic candidate. Once again, Buchanan hoped to wreck Stephen Douglas's chances of winning. Douglas was popular in the North and West, but largely despised in the South. Buchanan wanted the Democrats to choose someone who would keep the party united. Neither Douglas nor a fire-eater could do that.

In April the Democrats held a convention to choose their candidate. Douglas's supporters pushed through a platform that called for popular sovereignty. They did not want Congress or the Supreme Court to have control over slavery in the territories. Southern Democrats refused to accept this. Most now believed that territorial governments could not limit slavery in any way, even if voters called for it. They backed slave codes— federal laws that protected property, including slaves, in the territories. The delegates from most Southern states left the Democratic convention. Douglas was the choice of the delegates who remained, but under party rules he did not have enough votes to become the candidate.

The Democrats met again in June. The party was still split over the platform, even assuming the candidate would not be Douglas. Once again, most of the Southern delegates left, and this time they would not return. The remaining delegates then chose Douglas as their candidate, while the Southerners held their own convention. They selected Vice President John Breckinridge as their candidate and wrote a strong proslavery platform.

Buchanan backed Breckinridge and the Southerners, though a few years later he criticized the Southerners for having left the first convention. Had they stayed, Buchanan believed, the Dem-

Meanwhile, Buchanan prepared his last State of the Union address to Congress. The president once again blamed the anti-slavery forces of the North for interfering with the South's right to own slaves. Buchanan feared that Northern calls for abolition had stirred the slaves to seek their freedom more actively than in the past, leading Southerners to fear slave rebellions. That fear increased their distrust of the North, and of Lincoln in particular. But Buchanan said those fears did not give the South a legal right to secede. He deeply believed that no state could leave the Union unless the other states agreed. Secession was not a simple political act—it was revolutionary. "It may or it may not be a justifiable revolution, but still it is revolution." And in this case, Buchanan believed, the South had no reason to rebel.

Buchanan's message upset people on both sides of the issue. Most Southerners were angry that he did not acknowledge that they had a legal right to secede. Antislavery forces believed that the president had neither spoken strongly enough against secession nor made clear what he would to do stop it. One lawmaker said the address "was in all respects like the author, timid . . . in the face of slaveholding rebellion." Republicans across the country attacked the president's address, while many of his former Southern friends turned against him.

Buchanan's words did not have much impact in South Carolina. On December 20, 1860, it became the first state to secede. Several more Southern states soon followed. Buchanan had less than three months left in his presidency. They would be the most difficult months of his long career.

## TRYING TO PREVENT A WAR

Buchanan hoped that some compromise would settle the differences between the North and South over slavery in the territories.

At a minimum, he hoped to prevent more slave states from
seceding. Buchanan believed he
would need the support of at least
some of these states if war broke
out over secession. And he feared
that such a civil war would be long
and bloody. Congress did debate a
compromise. Senator John Crittenden of Kentucky brought up an
old idea—extend the Missouri
Compromise line (36°30') to the
Pacific Ocean. Another idea was
to let residents in Washington,
D.C. end slavery there, if Maryland and Virginia first abolished it.
Also, Crittenden said no future
law or amendment to the Constitution could end slavery where it
already existed.

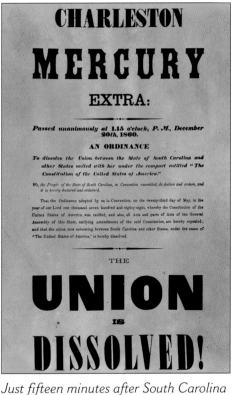

*Just fifteen minutes after South Carolina
voted to secede, a Charleston newspaper
published the news.*

On January 8, 1861, Buchanan expressed his support for
extending the old Missouri Compromise line. He also explained
that in any states that seceded, the federal government would
continue to collect taxes and perform other duties defined in the
Constitution. Such activities could lead to conflict with state officials. But Buchanan said he would not fire a first shot against the
Southerners. He wanted to avoid war. Still, his promise to fulfill
federal duties in the South could lead to violence. Alabama and
Florida had not seceded, but state officials had just seized federal
forts and an armory. South Carolina, though, was the true
hotspot of the growing struggle over secession.

# Defending Fort Sumter

Major Robert Anderson was in command of the federal troops at Fort Moultrie. He knew South Carolina was training its militia and preparing to take Moultrie and other federal forts in Charleston. After South Carolina seceded, state officials demanded that Buchanan turn the forts over to them, but Buchanan refused. State officials had told Buchanan they would not attack the fort if the president did not send reinforcements, in accordance with the president's statement that he would not send more troops for the time being.

Late in December 1860, Anderson moved all his troops to Fort Sumter, the newest of the forts in Charleston. It was still not finished, but if the South Carolinians were to attack, Sumter would be easier to defend. The move angered some members of Buchanan's cabinet. Anderson had not received specific orders to move, and his action was sure to upset the local officials. The

*Work to complete Fort Sumter went on while the confederates prepared to attack. Union soldiers added bricks to walls and moved cannons into position.*

remaining Southerners in the cabinet supported South Carolina's secession and wanted Buchanan to order Anderson back to Moultrie. The president agreed, which upset three newer members of the cabinet, Northerners who opposed secession. Moving Anderson back would leave him and his men open to attack. The Northerners said they would resign if Buchanan did not let Anderson stay at Sumter. Buchanan, despite his first impulse to support the Southern view, now agreed with the Northerners, whose support he did not want to lose.

A few days later, Buchanan gave the order to send reinforcements and supplies to Fort Sumter. Major Anderson said he did not need them. His message, however, did not reach the War Department until after the supply ship had sailed. When the ship reached Charleston, Southern cannons opened fire. The Union ship dipped its U.S. flag, a sign of distress. The Southern guns continued to fire until the ship turned back. Anderson did not use his fort's guns to help defend the Union ship because he did not have orders to attack the South Carolinians.

The failed relief of Fort Sumter upset people across the country. Northerners regarded the firing on the Union flag as an insult to the country, and thought that Buchanan had not done enough to protect the ship carrying reinforcements and to make sure it reached Charleston. Secessionists saw the move as an attack on South Carolina. The governor there demanded that Anderson turn over the fort, but he refused. The two men then reached a truce to halt further violence. Buchanan accepted the truce, as it gave him time to decide what to do next. Meanwhile, Anderson continued to strengthen his defenses at Fort Sumter, while the South Carolinians prepared to attack it. They would fight if Buchanan tried to send reinforcements again.

On February 6, Buchanan refused to turn over Fort Sumter to South Carolina. He claimed that only Congress had the power to give up federal property. Because Congress had not ceded the fort, however, Buchanan believed he had the legal duty to defend the the army post, and he was prepared to send reinforcements if Anderson asked for them. Even so, Buchanan had not challenged the takeover of other federal forts across the South.

## A NEW NATION

By this time, South Carolina was no longer an independent state. On February 4, six Southern states that had left the Union formed the Confederate States of America. Joining South Carolina were Alabama, Georgia, Mississippi, Florida, and Louisiana. Texas would soon enter the Confederacy, too, followed later by North Carolina, Virginia, Arkansas, and Tennessee.

## MOVING MESSAGES AND PEOPLE

As the Fort Sumter situation unfolded, President Buchanan did not have the benefit of constant and quick communication with Major Anderson or other military commanders. The telegraph, perfected in 1846, was the only form of long-distance communication. Electrical current was sent along metal wires. Turning the current on and off in set patterns reproduced letters of the alphabet, a system known as Morse code. In 1858

(continued)

Buchanan had helped introduce the newest breakthrough with the telegraph—messages sent across the Atlantic. The electrical current passed through a special cable placed on the ocean floor. Buchanan received a message from Great Britain's Queen Victoria. The telegraph, however, did not allow for totally private communication, so the president and his commanders did not like to use it.

Travel was also slow in 1860. The railroad was the only reliable form of long-distance travel, but trains pulled by steam engines could go no faster than about 25 miles per hour. Still, during Buchanan's years of public service, the United States had seen great growth in the railroad industry. The first passenger train ran in 1831. By 1850, the country had 9,000 miles of railroad track. That number tripled during the next ten years. The Civil War marked the first time trains played a major role in U.S. warfare. Both troops and supplies sometimes traveled by train.

*This map shows the Union and Confederate States at the beginning of the Civil War.*

The same day the Confederacy formed, a peace convention opened in Washington, D.C. Virginia had called for the convention, hoping to find a solution to the secession crisis. Buchanan said, "I hail this movement on the part of Virginia with great satisfaction." Delegates from twenty-one states attended, including representatives from seven slave states still in the Union. Congress, though, ignored the proposals that came from the convention, which largely followed the compromise suggested by Senator Crittenden of Kentucky. As the convention met, Confederate lawmakers told their president, Jefferson Davis, to take control of Fort Sumter—by force, if necessary.

In Washington, Buchanan and his cabinet heard rumors. Although Maryland and Virginia were still in the Union, both states had some citizens who favored secession. People said that secessionists might storm the capital city, take over the government, and make Vice President Breckinridge president. A Texas lawmaker had already suggested that Southerners kidnap Buchanan, so that the vice president could take control of the government. Buchanan called for several hundred troops to come to Washington, but the rumors of a secessionist takeover turned out to be false.

*Jefferson Davis served in the U.S. senate during most of Buchanan's presidency, before becoming president of the Confederacy.*

Buchanan also had battles with Congress. The legislature refused his requests for strengthening the military, even though Buchanan was not preparing to use force against the South. The Republicans in Congress also refused to take any direct steps against the South or give Buchanan more power to do so. Buchanan believed the Constitution did not give him more power to act. Yet, as he knew, other presidents before him had sometimes asserted powers not specifically spelled out in the Constitution. Buchanan refused to take such a step. It was against his personality, against his desire to prevent war. Buchanan's presidency drew to a close with no solution to the secession crisis and the threat of war growing.

# THE CIVIL WAR AND AFTER

As the secession crisis went on, Buchanan saw many of his old friends from the South turn against him. The Southerners in his cabinet left. One of them had created a scandal that further tainted Buchanan in Northern eyes. Secretary of War John Floyd had been caught misusing government funds. Buchanan acted slowly to get rid of Floyd, who had also illegally shipped to Southern states arms that would be used against the Union in the Civil War.

Other Southerners claimed that Buchanan was in contact with the Republicans and was doing what Lincoln wanted him to do. In truth, Buchanan was acting on his own, with the aid of his cabinet. The new members were from the North, but they were not Republicans. Like Buchanan, they wanted to keep the Union together. But with the failure of the Virginia Convention, the chance of compromise seemed to have vanished.

## THE OLD PRESIDENT AND THE NEW

Abraham Lincoln arrived in Washington on February 23 to prepare for his inauguration. He, his family, and some advisers had made the long trip from Illinois to the capital by train, so Lincoln could greet his supporters. The trip was a celebration, but it had its darker moments. Rumors spread that Lincoln might be killed as he traveled through Maryland. Although still in the Union, Maryland was a slave state, and some residents supported the Confederacy. Lincoln changed his plans, and traveled in disguise through Baltimore on his way to Washington.

*For most of his journey from Illinois to Washington, D.C., president-elect Abraham Lincoln was greeted by cheering crowds.*

Just hours after reaching the city, Lincoln surprised Buchanan by calling on him at the Executive Mansion. The president stopped a meeting with his cabinet to greet Lincoln and give him a tour of the mansion. Whatever his personal feelings about Lincoln and the Republicans, Buchanan treated Lincoln well during this short visit. Two days later, Buchanan returned the call, briefly meeting with Lincoln at his hotel.

With no new action in South Carolina or in Congress, Buchanan's last days as president were fairly quiet. He spent time with friends and officials who had worked for him. Following tradition, he moved out of the Executive Mansion on March 3, so the home could be prepared for the new president. Early the next morning, he received a letter from Major Anderson at Fort Sumter.

Although Charleston was calm, Anderson and his men were running out of supplies. The Union would have to send food or else turn over the fort to the Confederacy. Anderson guessed that the government would have to send 20,000 soldiers and a naval fleet to get through the Confederate forces surrounding Sumter. Their arrival would likely spark an attack on the fort and the reinforcements.

Buchanan might have read the note with some relief. Anderson's request required an important decision—risk war or give up the fort. But Buchanan would not be the one making the decision. In a few hours, he would pass that responsibility to the new president, Abraham Lincoln.

## Last Duties

March 4, 1861, started as a gray, dreary day in Washington, D.C. But as the morning went on the sun emerged through the clouds. Some 30,000 people gathered outside the Capitol for Lincoln's inauguration. Shortly after noon, Buchanan came by horse and carriage to Lincoln's hotel, and the two men rode together to the ceremony. Their carriage led a parade that filled the streets, complete with floats, marching bands, and soldiers. Armed soldiers also stood guard at certain spots in the capital. They would defend Lincoln from any violence meant to halt the inauguration.

No one knows for sure what the two men discussed as they rode through the cheering crowd. By one account, Buchanan said to Lincoln, "My dear sir, if you are as happy in entering the White House as I shall feel on returning to Wheatland, you are a happy man indeed."

Lincoln and Buchanan entered the Capitol arm in arm. *The New York Times*, which opposed Buchanan and his policies, said the fifteenth president looked "pale, sad, nervous." But the paper also said that the warm relation between the old president and the new "adds to the general tone of good feeling which prevails today."

On the night of the fourth and morning of the fifth of March, Buchanan held his last meetings with his former cabinet. They discussed Fort Sumter and Major Anderson's request.

The secretary of war prepared a letter for Lincoln, explaining the plans Buchanan had already made for sending reinforcements. Lincoln soon received that letter and Anderson's note. Buchanan then left Washington by train for Lancaster and his Wheatland home.

## The Decision Is Made

During the trip home, Buchanan made several stops along the way to greet voters who had supported him during his presidency. Residents of Baltimore warmly

*Crowds fill the streets of Washington, D.C., as Buchanan and Lincoln ride to the new president's inauguration.*

called for "Three cheers for Old Buck." York, Pennsylvania, held a parade for the only person from the state ever to reach the White House. Lancaster welcomed home its favorite son by firing guns and holding another parade.

Settling into his routine at Wheatland, Buchanan received reports from former cabinet members still in Washington. He also read newspapers from across the country. Most seemed to agree that Lincoln was following the course Buchanan had started, one that would avoid war. As late as April 10, Buchanan received a letter saying the troops at Fort Sumter would be withdrawn. Yet other friends wrote that Lincoln was under pressure from **radical** Republicans, who wanted the president to send the reinforcements.

In the end, Lincoln told the South Carolinians that supplies were on their way to Fort Sumter. If the Confederate forces did not prevent the arrival of the supplies, Lincoln would not send arms or reinforcements to Charleston. But the Confederate states would not let Anderson receive the supplies he needed. Instead, on the morning of April 12, 1861, Southern guns began firing on Fort Sumter. The war Buchanan had long feared had begun.

# FORT SUMTER

The troops fired their first shell around 4:30 AM. Soon, forty-three guns surrounding Sumter began to boom, one firing every two minutes. In the early morning hours, the Union troops lacked enough light to load and fire their heavy artillery. For several hours, they tried to hide from the incoming shells. Then, around 6:30, the Union cannons fired back. The firing lasted through the day and began again the next morning.

Finally, at 1:30 on April 13, Anderson surrendered. The South Carolinians took control of the fort the next day. As the Civil War went on, the Union tried to retake the fort but failed. In February 1865, with the war almost over, Union troops managed to enter Charleston and take back Sumter.

# The War at Wheatland

Buchanan blamed the start of the war on the South. He had warned Southerners that attacking Sumter would bring a Union military response. Lincoln did not delay in preparing that response. He called 75,000 volunteers to join the Union Army. Across the North, thousands of young men eagerly answered the call. They believed they could quickly and easily defeat the South as they supported the Union.

Buchanan soon noticed a change among his Lancaster neighbors, especially the Republicans. Some warned him not to come into town anymore. Others sent nasty letters or left notes threatening to burn down his home. Republicans were stirring up the idea that Buchanan should take the blame for starting the war. One newspaper said that Andrew Jackson would have had the will to end the rebellion before it ever spread. Buchanan, the paper believed, had not been a strong president. As the months went on, even Lincoln joined in. He suggested that Buchanan's actions had weakened the Union or made it easier for the South to secede.

Some friends remained loyal, as local Masons promised to guard his home day and night. And the former president tried to defend himself in a letter to a local newspaper. That only stirred more anger among the growing anti-Buchanan forces in the area.

Early in 1862, a leading Republican published an article that once again upset Buchanan. It described a heated cabinet meeting that had taken place in February 1861. Since the article was largely false. Buchanan asked several of his former advisers to publicly attack the article and defend him. They refused, not wanting to upset Lincoln and Republican Party leaders.

## BATTLING A GENERAL

Out of office, Buchanan had a war of words with General Winfield Scott, who had been commander of the U.S Army in 1860. Just before the election, Scott wrote a letter that said states had a right to secede. He also advised Buchanan to send more troops to forts in the South, in case states did secede. Buchanan, who disliked Scott, he ignored the advice. Buchanan came to believe that Scott's views encouraged the South to secede. In 1862 the two men exchanged public letters debating what had happened before and right after Lincoln took office. Scott had given the new president misleading information about Buchanan, which Lincoln then repeated in public. Buchanan defended his actions during the secession crisis, correcting some of the inaccuracies in Scott's letter. Scott was forced to acknowledge his mistakes, and Buchanan had his first "victory" in trying to get out the truth about his presidency.

Buchanan was disappointed, but not surprised. He knew that the only way to stop the lies being spread about his presidency was to present the facts as he knew them. He began writing a book, which was not published until 1866.

While Buchanan worked on his book, the Civil War dragged on. In late June 1863, Confederate general Robert E. Lee invaded Pennsylvania, reaching the area around Gettysburg. Fearing the battle to come, friends told Buchanan he should leave Wheatland. Buchanan sent his niece Harriet to Philadelphia, but he remained at his home. Confederate troops came within about ten miles of Wheatland, and on July 1 the Battle of Gettysburg began. Both sides suffered huge losses, but the North won, ending Lee's invasion of the North. Buchanan later wrote, "I felt no alarm at the approach of the rebels . . . and should not have removed from Wheatland had I been sur- rounded by a hundred thousand of them." Now In his seventies, Buchanan had learned to accept any "evils" that came in life.

*Combined, the North and South suffered more than 50,000 casualties during the three-day Battle of Gettysburg.*

## POLITICS OF THE DAY

During the war, Buchanan remained interested in politics. He exchanged letters with lawmakers in Washington and with some of his former cabinet members. They discussed the issues of the day, as well as the bad treatment Buchanan received in the news- papers. In Pennsylvania, he disagreed with some Democrats who opposed the war. Buchanan said Lincoln had done the right thing, once Sumter was attacked, and loyal Northerners should support the president. He wrote in September 1861, "This is the moment for action; for prompt, energetic and united action; and not for discussion of peace." The North had to reunite the country.

As the war went on, Democrats resisted Lincoln's efforts to draft more soldiers. They thought Lincoln had violated the Con- stitution when he took away some of the legal rights of the Rebels and the Northerners who supported them. Buchanan also thought Lincoln sometimes used powers not granted to the president by the Constitution. But he never attacked the president in public. And he always supported Lincoln's goal of fighting to bring the South back into the Union. During the 1864 presidential election, some Democrats called for peace talks with the South if their candidate won. Buchanan opposed the idea. Yet after Lincoln won reelection, Buchanan thought the president should talk with the Confederacy. By now, a Union victory seemed clear. Lincoln could agree to take the seceding states back, "leaving the slavery issue to settle itself." Buchanan believed the two sides would soon come to respect each other. As before, he did not understood the hatred that still existed on both sides.

# THE EMANCIPATION PROCLAMATION

On January 1, 1863, President Lincoln issued the Emancipation Proclamation. Lincoln freed slaves in areas of Confederate states not under Union military control. No Southern slaves were actually freed because of Lincoln's action. The proclamation also did not free slaves in the so-called border states that had not left the Union: Missouri, Delaware, Maryland, and Kentucky. Lincoln's statement, however, did let free blacks join the military. And it gave Americans the sense that the war was now about ending slavery, not just keeping the Union together. That thought thrilled abolitionists but angered some Northern Democrats and slaveholders in the border states. Buchanan opposed the proclamation, but he once again refrained from public criticism of the president's policies.

# LAST YEARS

The last Union victories and the end of the war in April 1865 made Buchanan happy. But he, like most of the North, was stunned by the news of Lincoln's murder on April 15, 1865. Buchanan respected Lincoln and thought he would have done well in repairing relations between the North and South. Vice President Andrew Johnson would now have that important task. Buchanan knew Johnson from his Washington days, and Johnson had

*James Buchanan, photographed toward the end of his political career.*

once visited him at Wheatland. Although Buchanan thought the new president had the skills to do a good job, Johnson actually had a disastrous presidency and was impeached by the House of Representatives.

In the months after the war, Buchanan wrote that he was enjoying himself. He was in good health, considering his age, and his life was peaceful. He completed his book, *Mr. Buchanan's Administration on the Eve of the Rebellion*. He believed it showed that he had done the best he could have during his presidency. Buchanan never questioned his decisions of those years. And he blamed Congress for not passing laws that would have helped him end the secession crisis.

Buchanan's health began to weaken in 1867, and the following spring he developed a severe cold. The cold turned into pneumonia, and Buchanan could not recover. He died on June 1, 1868, with many relatives by his side.

Buchanan had hoped his book would prove his presidency was a good one. But for the most part, historians have not seen his presidency in a favorable light. Some take the view of

Republicans of the 1850s, who thought Buchanan always favored the South in the legal battles over slavery. Buchanan was not proslavery, but his view of the Constitution and his personal relations with many Southerners did shape his policies. Slavery was legal, and so he thought it wrong to abolish the practice. Only an amendment to the Constitution could end it. (That amendment, the thirteenth, was ratified in December 1865.)

In recent years, a number of historians have called Buchanan one of the worst presidents ever. A few say he was the worst. In her 2004 biography of him, Jean Baker says he came close to committing treason "in his betrayal of the national trust" and his preference for the South. Buchanan consistently failed to see how his policies divided the nation and his own party. His faith in his own ideas and values—some would say his arrogance—kept him from seeing the perspective of abolitionists, Stephen Douglas, Republicans, and others who did not share his views. Yet some historians say he took a strong stance against South Carolina in December 1860. Lincoln basically followed his plans. Yet Lincoln was more willing to fight than Buchanan was. And Buchanan most likely would not have used the war to end slavery, as Lincoln eventually did.

Buchanan became president at one of the most difficult times in the country's history. Slavery was the main issue during Buchanan's political career. The strong emotions over it made compromise impossible. His defense of slavery—and the notion of states' rights versus the power of the federal government—largely defined his presidency. Today, any defense of slavery would be untolerable. But Buchanan grew up and lived during a time when many whites accepted the practice. Other whites opposed slavery, but did not support equal rights for free blacks. The country still wrestles with the racism that shaped Buchanan's age.

*Despite his intelligence and political skills, Buchanan sometimes acted unwisely in the years before the Civil War, leading to his low opinion among modern historians.*

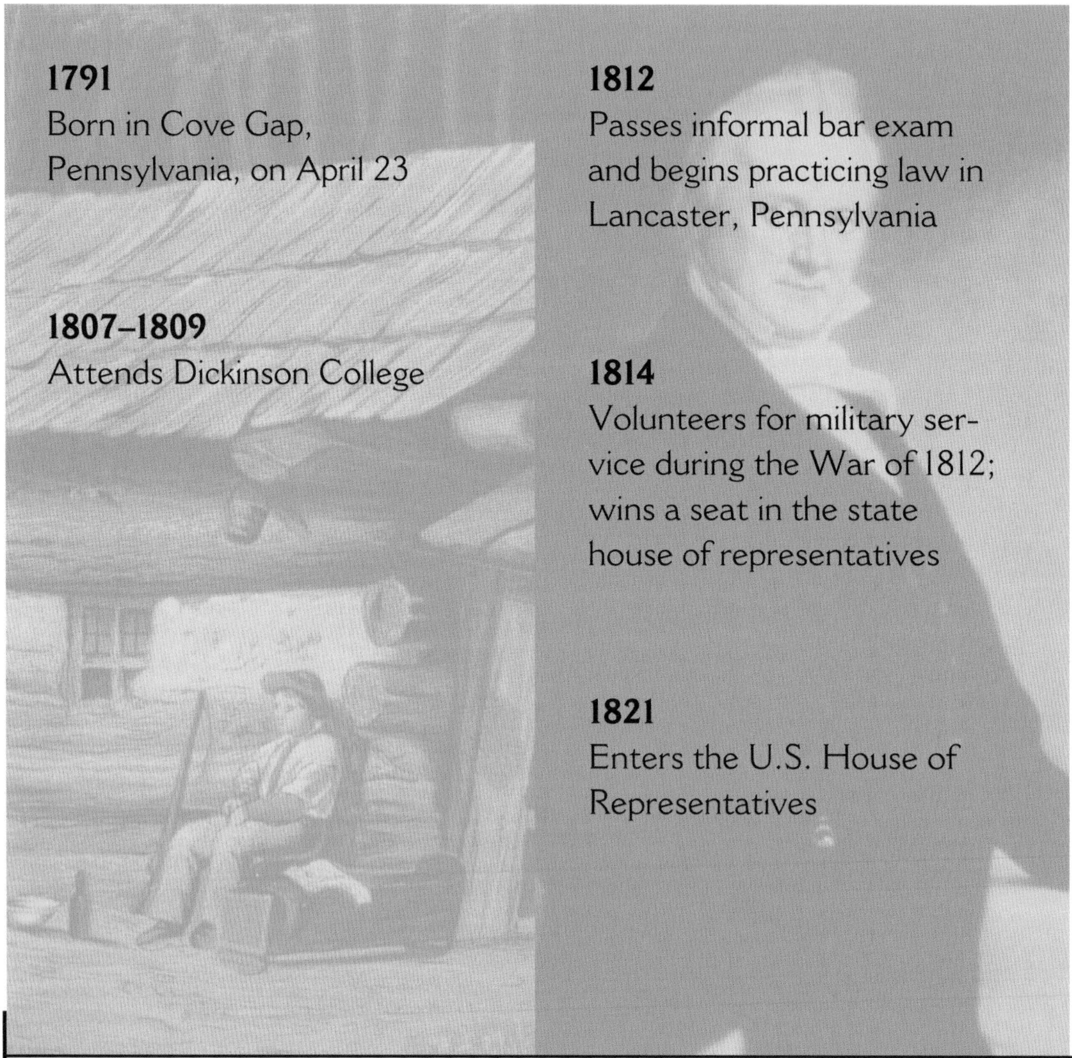

**1791**
Born in Cove Gap,
Pennsylvania, on April 23

**1807–1809**
Attends Dickinson College

**1812**
Passes informal bar exam
and begins practicing law in
Lancaster, Pennsylvania

**1814**
Volunteers for military service during the War of 1812;
wins a seat in the state
house of representatives

**1821**
Enters the U.S. House of
Representatives

**1790**

**1832–1833**
Serves as U.S. minister to
Russia

**1834**
Enters the U.S. Senate

**1845–1849**
Serves as secretary of state
under President James K. Polk

**1855–1856**
Serves as the U.S. minister
to Great Britain

**1857–1861**
Serves as fifteenth president
of the United States

**1868**
Dies at Wheatland, his
home in Lancaster,
Pennsylvania, on June 1

**1870**

**CHAPTER ONE**

p.7, "Love for the Constitution . . . American people." James Buchanan, "Inaugural Address," 4 March 1857. Online at The American Presidency Project, <http://www.presidency.ucsb.edu/ws/index.php?pid=25817>. (Accessed 9 March 2009)

p.7, "The specific powers . . . possible emergency." James Buchanan, *Mr. Buchanan's Administration on the Eve of the Rebellion*. New York: D. Appleton and Company, 1866, pp. iii–iv.

p.9, "Excited [my] ambition . . . useful to their country." James Buchanan, quoted in Jean H. Baker, *James Buchanan*. New York: Times Books, 2004, p. 11.

p.11, "To be considered . . . mischief." James Buchanan, quoted in Philip Shriver Klein, *President James Buchanan: A Biography*. University Park, PA: The Pennsylvania State University Press, 1962, p. 9.

p.17, "Feel & act more as a Nation . . . better secured." Albert Gallatin, quoted in Thomas G. Paterson et al. *American Foreign Relations: A History. Volume 1: To 1920.* Boston: Houghton Mifflin, 2000, p. 79.

p.18, "Without money in the treasury . . . other in the world." James Buchanan, "Fourth of July Oration," 4 July 1815. In *The Works of James Buchanan*, James B. Moore, ed. Vol. 1, p. 4. Dickinson College Digital Collection, <http://deila.dickinson.edu/cdm4/document.php?CISOROOT=/buchan&CISOPTR=4513&REC=7>. (Accessed 10 March 2009)

**CHAPTER TWO**

p.23, "Let not your passions . . . sober judgment." James Buchanan Sr., quoted in Klein, *President James Buchanan: A Biography*, p. 36.

p.24, "The reputation . . . it deserves." James Buchanan, quoted in Klein, *President James Buchanan: A Biography*, p. 39.

p.24, "No trace . . . between Federal and Democrat." James Buchanan, quoted in Baker, *James Buchanan*, p. 23.

p.26, "I called upon General Jackson . . . any other person." James Buchanan, quoted in Klein, *President James Buchanan: A Biography*, p. 57.

p.28, "For my own part . . . the South." James Buchanan, quoted in George T. Curtis, *Life of James Buchanan*, New York: Harper Brothers, 1883, vol. I, p. 68.

p.29, "Inept busybody." Andrew Jackson, quoted in Baker, *James Buchanan*, p. 31.

p.29, "I was leaving a city . . . never abandoned me." James Buchanan, quoted in Curtis, *Life of James Buchanan*, vol. I, p. 136.

p.30, "I think it more than probable . . . my happiness." James Buchanan, quoted in Curtis, *Life of James Buchanan*, vol. I, p. 206.

## Chapter Three

p.32, "Dangerous to the rights . . . people of the Union." James Buchanan, letter to F. R. Shunk et al., 30 June 1836. In Works, vol. 3, p. 117. <http://deila.dickinson.edu/cdm4/document.php?CISOROOT=/buchan&CISOPTR=4515&REC=12>. (Accessed 18 July 2009)

p.33, "Inconsistent . . . was founded." Andrew Jackson, "Proclamation to the People of South Carolina," in *Annals of America*, Chicago: Encyclopedia Britannica, 1968, vol. 5, p. 588.

p.34, "Desperate fanatics . . . ignorant enthusiasts." James Buchanan, quoted in Curtis, *Life of James Buchanan*, vol. I, pp. 315, 318.

p.35, "No government . . . this right." James Buchanan, quoted in Curtis, *Life of James Buchanan*, vol. I, p. 321.

p.39, "A great and glorious mission . . . fulfill our destiny." James Buchanan, quoted in Baker, *James Buchanan*, p. 35.

p.41, "Has been selfish . . . public questions." James Polk, quoted in *James Buchanan and the Political Crisis of the 1850s*. Michael J. Birkner, ed. Selinsgrove, PA: Susquehanna University Press, 1996, p. 27.

## Chapter Four

p.46, "That in four years . . . two republics." James Buchanan, quoted in Klein, *President James Buchanan: A Biography*, p. 213.

p.47, "After a long and stormy . . . without regret." James Buchanan, letter to General Porter, 4 June 1852. In *Works*, vol. 8, p. 451. <http://deila.dickinson.edu/cdm4/document.php?CISOROOT=/buchan&CISOPTR=9147&REC=17>. (Accessed 23 March 2009)

p.48, "In the simple dress of an American citizen." William L. Marcy, quoted in Klein, *President James Buchanan: A Biography*, p. 228.

p.50, "Non-interference by Congress . . . District of Columbia. 1856 Democratic Platform, quoted in James A. Rawley, "Stephen A. Douglas and the Kansas-Nebraska Act." *The Nebraska-Kansas Act of 1854*. John R. Wunder and Joann M. Ross, eds. Lincoln: University of Nebraska Press, 2008, p. 76.

p.50, "Too long distracted . . . dangerous excitement." James Buchanan, letter to Committee of Notification, 16 June 1856, In *Works*, vol. 10, pp. 82, 83. <http://deila.dickinson.edu/cdm4/document.php?CISOROOT=/buchan&CISOPTR=9149&REC=8>. (Accessed 6 April 2009)

p.52, "Permit our Southern neighbors to manage their own domestic affairs." James Buchanan, quoted in Baker, *James Buchanan*, p. 74.

p.52, "Agitation . . . destroy sectional parties." James Buchanan, letter to Mr. Mason, 29 December 1856. In *Works*, vol. 10, p 100. <http://deila.dickinson.edu/cdm4/document.php?CISOROOT=/buchan&CISOPTR=9149&REC=8>. (Accessed 7 April 2009)

p.55, "To their decision . . . whatever this may be." James Buchanan, "Inaugural Address."

## CHAPTER FIVE

p.58, "Protect it from the violence . . . rule or ruin." James Buchanan, *Mr. Buchanan's Administration*, p. 31.

p.58, "If Kansas comes in . . . inflict it." Thomas Thomas, quoted in Baker, *James Buchanan*, p. 97.

p.59, "Mr. President . . . Jackson is dead." Stephen A. Douglas, quoted in Elbert B. Smith, *The Presidency of James Buchanan*. Lawrence: The University Press of Kansas, 1975. p. 41.

p.61, "Cotton is king." James Henry Hammond, "On the Admission of Kansas, Under the Lecompton Constitution." Speech delivered 4 March 1858. Online at America's Civil War, <http://www.sewanee.edu/faculty/Willis/Civil_War/documents/HammondCotton.html>. (Accessed 12 April 2009)

p.61, "The suffering and distress . . . power to extend relief." James Buchanan, "First Annual Message to Congress on the State of the Union," 8 December 1857. Online at The American Presidency Project, <http://www.presidency.ucsb.edu/ws/index.php?pid=29498>. (Accessed 12 April 2009)

p.62, "There is no starving . . . than in the whole South." James Henry Hammond, "On the Admission of Kansas, Under the Lecompton Constitution."

p.64, "A stubborn old gentleman, very fond of having his own way." Jeremiah Black, quoted in Klein, *President James Buchanan: A Biography*, p. 285.

p.66, "I do not recognize the right of anybody to expel me from the Democratic Party!" Stephen A. Douglas, quoted in Bruce Chadwick, *1858: Abraham Lincoln, Jefferson Davis, Robert E. Lee, Ulysses S. Grant and the War They Failed to See*. Naperville, IL: Sourcebooks, 2008, p. 91.

p.67, "So great that it is almost absurd." James Buchanan, quoted in Smith, *The Presidency of James Buchanan*, p. 81.

p.68, "Resistance to lawful authority . . . disastrous to its authors." James Buchanan, "Second Annual Message to Congress on the State of the Union," 6 December 1858. Online at The American Presidency Project, <http://www.presidency.ucsb.edu/ws/index.php?pid=29499>. (Accessed 13 April 2009)

## CHAPTER SIX

p.69, "The demon spirit . . . alive in the land." James Buchanan, "Third Annual Message to Congress on the State of the Union," 19 December 1859. Online at The American Presidency Project, <http://www.presidency.ucsb.edu/ws/index.php?pid=29500>. (Accessed 14 April, 2009)

p.73, "I see no possibility . . . consider it desirable." John Slidell, quoted in Klein, *President James Buchanan: A Biography*, p. 352.

p.74, "It may or it may not be a justifiable revolution, but still it is revolution." James Buchanan, "Fourth Annual Message to Congresson the State of the Union," 6 December 1858. Online at The American Presidency Project, <http://www.presidency.ucsb.edu/ws/index.php?pid=29499>. (Accessed 15 April 2009)

p.74, "Was in all respects . . . slaveholding rebellion." Charles Francis Adams, quoted in Harold Holzer, *Lincoln President-Elect: Abraham Lincoln and the Great Secession Winter 1860–1861*. New York: Simon & Schuster, 2008, p. 131.

p.80, "I hail this movement . . . with great satisfaction." James Buchanan, "Special Message," 28 January 1861. Online at The American Presidency Project, <http://www.presidency.ucsb.edu/ws/index.php?pid=68454>. (Accessed 15 April 2009)

## CHAPTER SEVEN

p.84, "My dear sir . . . a happy man indeed." James Buchanan, quoted in Klein, *President James Buchanan: A Biography*, p. 402.

p.84, "Pale, sad, nervous . . . which prevails today." "Our Washington Dispatches." *The New York Times*, 5 March 1861, p. 1.

p.85, "Three cheers for Old Buck." Baltimore crowd, quoted in Klein, *President James Buchanan: A Biography*, p. 403.

p.89, "I felt no alarm . . . a hundred thousand of them." James Buchanan, quoted in Klein, *President James Buchanan: A Biography*, p. 423.

p.89, "This is the moment for action . . . not for discussion of peace." James Buchanan, quoted in Curtis, *Life of James Buchanan*, vol. 2, p. 566.

p.90, "Leaving the slavery issue to settle itself." James Buchanan, quoted in Curtis, *Life of James Buchanan*, vol. 2, p. 629.

p.92, "In his betrayal of the national trust." Jean Baker, *James Buchanan*, p. 142.

# GLOSSARY

**abolitionists** people who seek an immediate end to a practice, such as slavery

**annex** take control of a bordering country or other land

**armory** place where weapons are made or stored

**cabinet** the heads of different government departments who advise a president

**charter** document issued by a government to a group of people that allows them to form a company or other organization

**Democratic Republican Party** early political party led by Thomas Jefferson that stressed the rights of the states versus the federal government and promoted the interests of farmers

**Electoral College** political representatives from each state whose votes decide presidential elections. Each state receives the same number of electors as the number of people it sends to Congress.

**emancipation** the act of freeing one or more slaves

**Federalists** early political party led by Alexander Hamiliton that supported a strong national government to help merchants and foreign trade

**functionary** person who holds a political office or government job

**impeachment** legal process for determining whether an elected official or judge broke the law and should be removed from office

**indentured servants** people who sign a contract agreeing to work for someone else for a certain number of years, receiving room and board in return

**Louisiana Purchase** Roughly 524 million acres of land, stretching from the Mississippi River to the Rocky Mountains, sold by France to the United States in 1803.

**militia** military force made up of civilians who only serve during times of crisis

**nullify** declare to be not valid or to no longer be in effect

**petitions** requests to the government to carry out some action, or the actual documents making those requests

**radical** extreme in thought or actions

**secession** the act of breaking away from a country or other political state

**Union** another name for the United States; especially used to refer to the North during the Civil War

# BOOKS

*Annals of America*. Chicago: Encyclopedia Britannica Press, 1968.

Baker, Jean H. *James Buchanan*. New York: Times Books, 2004.

Binder, Frederick Moore. *James Buchanan and the American Empire*. Selinsgrove, PA: Susquehanna University Press, 1994.

Birkner, Michael J., ed. *James Buchanan and the Political Crisis of the 1850s*. Selinsgrove, PA: Susquehanna University Press, 1996.

Blight, David W. *Passages to Freedom: The Underground Railroad in History and Memory*. Washington, DC: Smithsonian Books, 2004.

Blum, John M., et al. *The National Experience: A History of the United States*. 4th ed. New York: Harcourt Brace Jovanovich, 1977.

Borneman, Walter R. *1812: The War That Forged a Nation*. New York: HarperCollins, 2004.

Brands, H. W. *Andrew Jackson: His Life and Times*. New York: Anchor Books, 2006.

Buchanan, James. *Mr. Buchanan's Administration on the Eve of the Rebellion*. New York: D. Appleton and Company, 1866.

Chadwick, Bruce. *1858: Abraham Lincoln, Jefferson Davis, Robert E. Lee, Ulysses S. Grant and the War They Failed to See*. Naperville, IL: Sourcebooks, 2008.

Curtis, George T. *Life of James Buchanan*. 2 vols. New York: Harper Brothers, 1883.

Detzer, David. *Allegiance: Fort Sumter, Charleston, and the Beginning of the Civil War*. San Diego: Harvest Book/Harcourt, 2002.

Finkelman, Paul. *Dred Scott v. Sandford: A Brief History with Documents*. Boston: Bedford Books, 1997.

Freehling, William W. *The Road to Disunion. Volume II: Secessionists Triumphant 1854-1861*. New York: Oxford University Press, 2007.

Foner, Eric, and Garraty, John A., eds. *The Reader's Companion to American History*. Boston: Houghton Mifflin, 1990.

Holt, Michael F. *The Fate of Their Country: Politicians, Slavery Extension, and the Coming of the Civil War*. New York: Hill and Wang, 2004.

Holzer, Harold. *Lincoln President-Elect: Abraham Lincoln and the Great Secession Winter 1860–1861*. New York: Simon & Schuster, 2008.

Kelley, Robert L. *The Cultural Pattern in American Politics*. New York: Knopf, 1979.

Klein, Philip Shriver. *President James Buchanan: A Biography*. University Park, PA: The Pennsylvania State University Press, 1962.

Lord, Walter. *The Dawn's Early Light*. Baltimore: The Johns Hopkins University Press, 1972.

Moore, John B., ed. *The Works of James Buchanan*. Various volumes. Available online at http://deila.dickinson.edu/cdm4/browse.php?CISOROOT=%2Fbuchan

Nagel, Paul C. *John Quincy Adams: A Public Life, a Private Life*. New York, Knopf, 1997.

Painter, Nell Irvin. *Creating Black Americans: African-American History and Its Meanings, 1619 to the Present*. New York: Oxford University Press, 2006.

Paterson, Thomas G., et al. *American Foreign Relations: A History. Volume 1: To 1920*. Boston: Houghton Mifflin, 2000.

Schneider, Dorothy, and Carl J. Schneider. *An Eyewitness History of Slavery in America: From Colonial Times to the Civil War*. New York: Checkmark Books, 2001.

Smith, Elbert B. *The Presidency of James Buchanan*. Lawrence: The University Press of Kansas, 1975.

Wunder, John R., and Joann M. Ross, eds. *The Nebraska-Kansas Act of 1854*. Lincoln: University of Nebraska Press, 2008.

# NEWSPAPER

"Our Washington Dispatches." *The New York Times*, March 5, 1861, p. 1.

# WEBSITES

www.albanach.org/ulster.html

www.lecomptonkansas.com/index.php?doc=time.php

www.territorialkansasonline.org/~imlskto/cgi-bin/index.php?SCREEN=timeline

www.slaveryinamerica.org/history/hs_es_cotton.htm

http://deila.dickinson.edu/buchanan/timeline/1809_1820.htm

http://millercenter.org/academic/americanpresident/Buchanan

www.phmc.state.pa.us/ppet/buchanan/page1.asp?secid=31

www.firstladies.org/biographies/firstladies.aspx?biography=16

http://elections.harpweek.com/1860/cartoon-1860-Medium.
 asp?UniqueID=45&Year=

Tolson, Jay. "The 10 Worst Presidents." *U.S. News & World Report*,
 February 16, 2007. Available at http://www.usnews.com/articles/
 news/history/2007/02/16/worst-presidents-james-buchanan.html.
 Accessed on April 6, 2009.

Plus websites cited above and in end notes for source of quotes.

# ABOUT THE AUTHOR

A history graduate of the University of Connecticut, freelance author Michael Burgan has written more than 150 fiction and nonfiction books for children.